THE LOST VILLAGE

The Lost Village

Rural Life Between the Wars

RALPH WHITLOCK

Robert Hale Limited
Clerkenwell House
Clerkenwell Green
London EC1R 0HT

British Library Cataloguing in Publication Data

Whitlock, Ralph
    The lost village : rural life between
    the Wars.
    1. Wiltshire. Pitton. Social life,
    1911-1950. Personal observations
    I. Title
    942.3'19

    ISBN 0-7090-3281-1

Photoset in North Wales by
Derek Doyle & Associates, Mold, Clwyd.
Printed in Great Britain by
St Edmundsbury Press Ltd, Bury St Edmunds, Suffolk.
Bound by Hunter & Foulis Ltd.

Contents

Illustrations

Christmas greetings from Elsie Whitlock and her fellow
   Salvation Army officer
Cows dragging their way up White Hill on a frosty
   morning
Tom Collins and his son Sam in the early 1920s
Ted Whitlock with Gipsy in 1918
Lavender Cottage, the original farmhouse of Taylor's Farm
Emily Mills at Pond Cottage, *c.*1920

Between pages 128 and 129
Threshing in the Thirties
Pitton's first tractor
Threshing with an old-type steam engine
The Pitton Sheep Shearing Gang
Isaac Dear surrounded by sheep cribs
Downland milking bail, *c.*1946
Walt Parsons enjoying a quiet smoke
Ted Whitlock with a lively calf
Rick making, *c.*1939
Ted Mills, tractor-driver
Charlie Whitlock claiming to be a poacher!
Cutting grass for hay

All photographs except 'Cutting grass for hay' from the
collection of the author. Chapter head illustrations and
maps by Roger Pearce.

Acknowledgements

The author extends his best thanks to Roger Pearce for providing the illustrations for the chapter heads and for the maps, and also to old friends of his boyhood who checked his reminiscences and augmented them with their own.

Preface

A way of life enjoyed or endured by nearly a thousand generations in the lovely countryside of England moved into its last phase in the three decades between the wars. Now it has vanished for ever. No cataclysm of nature has obliterated the villages which were its setting, nor has the pageant of the seasons changed its majestic cycle. The Biblical promise that, 'While the earth remaineth, summer and winter, and cold and heat, and day and night shall not cease' still holds good, but the other clause in the covenant, 'seedtime and harvest', means little to the present descendants of that long chain of ancestors. Summer is now the season for taking a holiday, not for gathering a harvest.

As memories of that lost way of life fade into the mists, it is important that they should be recorded before they are entirely lost. In an age when archaeology strives more enthusiastically and more efficiently than ever before to disinter traces of the past, it would be incongruous to allow the living repositories of ancient traditions to take their information to the oblivion of the grave.

It was therefore a joy to me to be invited to write a study in depth of life in an English village between the First and Second World Wars. Out of the thousands of villages which could have been chosen for the survey, the choice was made for me by the fact that the village in which I was born and reared could hardly have been bettered for the purpose. Here I was presented to the world six months before the First World War began and here I have lived for most of the years since. Here too I have been able to tap the recollections of my contemporaries and to have access to virtually all documentary sources that exist (not that they amount to very much).

One other advantage was granted me. As the son of middle-aged parents (who had been married for twelve years before I was born), I was brought up in a family where mealtime conversation tended to dwell on the past. By the time I left school, I felt I knew as much about the village of forty years earlier as I did of the contemporary one. And subsequent training as an historian of the countryside helped me to fit local events into their broader context.

Although Pitton epitomizes the multitudinous villages that spangle the English landscape, it is perhaps better suited than most to illustrate the peasant economy of the countryside from the time when men first began to grow crops and milk cows. For it was essentially a peasant village, a village of small farmers and cottagers unaffected by the influence of resident squire and parson. Left largely to its own devices, its life uncomplicated by such distractions as telephone, piped water, electricity and wireless, and isolated from other villages and from the nearest town (six miles distant) by lanes with atrocious surfaces, it preserved a heritage of customs and mental attitudes from a remote ancestry.

The year 1912 is taken as a base line, for the reason that it saw a sale of property involving the entire parish. The absentee landowner in distant Dorset divested himself of the estate, giving the villagers the opportunity to acquire for themselves the land which they and their ancestors had farmed and the houses in which they had lived for generations. As the narrative unfolds, it becomes necessary from time to time to refer back to 'the Sale'.

After the Sale, though, the 1914-18 War followed so quickly that the old ways of life did not appreciably change until the 1920s. The pace was accelerating when hostilities were resumed in 1939. Our study therefore takes note of what was time-honoured and traditional in the early part of the period and then examines how new pressures forced it to evolve and adapt.

Now the ideas that seemed so novel and even daring in

the 1920s have been swept into obsolescence. The village of that first decade after the 1914-18 War seems to the new residents of the countryside as remote and incomprehensible as the village perched in Roman times on the downs overlooking the Pitton valley.

One feels that the villagers of the 1920s would have been more at home up there in, say, the year 288 than they would in the Pitton of 1988. Transported back some 1,700 years, they would, of course, have found it strange to be living on the hill instead of in the valley, and no doubt the different background of family, social and religious life would have worried them at first, but they would soon have forged a link with the men who were skilled with the same tools and the women who followed the same domestic routine as theirs. They would quickly have become immersed in the familiar country rhythm of ploughing and sowing, haymaking and harvest, milking, lambing and shearing. The seasons would in their appointed cycle bring the usual ordeals of frost and drought, of blizzards in winter and storms in harvest. They would soon be exchanging notes with those remote ancestors who, somehow, would not seem all that remote, pointing out certain tasks which they had learned to perform more efficiently and picking up useful features of ancient lore long since forgotten.

But transport those same villagers, men and women who were elderly in the 1920s, into the world of the 1980s and they would be bewildered, lost. How could they adapt to roads congested with speeding cars (and not a horse in sight!), to a television screen in every house, to supermarkets packed with unrecognizable or unheard-of goods, to telephones ringing, to instant hot water out of taps, to microwave ovens in place of the stockpot over the hearth fire, to jet planes and helicopters overhead, to strangers everywhere ... Their reaction would be that of old Noah White on his first visit to the seaside (as described on page 101). Words would fail them. They would look around uncomprehendingly, switch off their minds and plead, 'Take me home.'

1 Pitton in its Place

The undulating chalk downs of Salisbury Plain, that once
uncannily resembled a petrified grey-green ocean, pile up
in a final wave against the viscid, clayey shores of the
Hampshire Basin. In the south-eastern corner of Wiltshire
the last scarp of the downs almost coincides with a section
of the Wiltshire/Hampshire boundary, forming a ridge of
hills that runs parallel to the Stockbridge-Salisbury road,
the A30. Past the Pheasant Inn, as the traveller speeds
towards Salisbury, the road swerves away to the right and
away from Pitton's secluded valley.

From the Pheasant a lane following the valley floor leads
straight into the compact village. Known as Bottom Way,

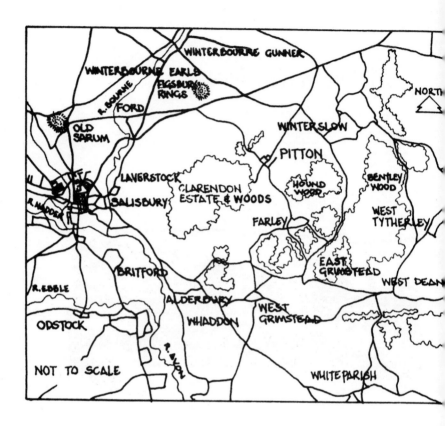

the lane is indeed the only road to give level access to Pitton. The other approaches descend steep, winding hills, sunk between high banks which ensure they get blocked by every heavy snowfall. How long does it take for farm carts to carve out a sunken way two or three feet deep? A foot a century? Probably so, on a fairly steep gradient, though longer on level ground.

Pitton is the last downland village in this corner of Wiltshire. The heaving plain rolls away to limitless horizons to the north. Curving in a broad arc to the west, south and south-east and creeping to the very brow of the hill are the woods, extensive and secret even today but now only the fragmented vestiges of the ancient Forest of Penchet, which in early times covered much of the territory between the New Forest and the Thames Valley. Its Celtic or Roman-British name testifies to its antiquity, though later names have been attached to most of its now independent sectors – Melchet, Clarendon, Harewood, Doles.

Like other villages along the forest fringe, old-time Pitton had a dual character. Though primarily agricultural, it also had a strong bias towards the woods, and woodland industries flourished. The north-east wind, howling along Bottom Way, was halted by an abrupt barrier – a line of tall elms standing like sentries in a straight line across the entire breadth of the valley. In 1930 a ferocious gale uprooted them all, thus forestalling Dutch elm disease. On the lower side of the village, however, the dwellings were drawn out towards the woods.

In the period to be reviewed in this book there were three cottages a quarter of a mile out of the village on the footpath called Cold Harbour. Two others stood, one on either side of the lane, at the far end of Slateway, while just around the corner, at the foot of Dunley Hill, the ruins of yet another woodman's cottage, with snowdrops in the garden, provided a play place for children still living. The entrance to the Clarendon Estate was guarded by a keeper's cottage, and half a mile into the woods stood more houses, unimaginatively though accurately known as Four Cottages. Until about 1880 the Clarendon Woods extended to the higher end of White Way, the Salisbury road. This coppice, known as Shreaves Wood, provided a site for another cottage, occupied sometimes by a keeper, sometimes by a woodman. The well which supplied the householder with water was still intact a few years ago.

Pitton can thus be seen as essentially a forest village, and that is the key to its story. It is not mentioned in Domesday Book because it was included in the Royal Forest of Clarendon, which had been created from part of ancient Penchet. A footpath of about 2½ miles through the present Clarendon Woods, *en route* to Salisbury, skirts the site of Clarendon Palace, a royal hunting lodge for some four medieval centuries. Here a succession of monarchs took their leisure in a virtually unfortified, straggling site of about eighteen acres – almost unique in an age of strong castles. During the 1930s a series of summer excavations, brought to an untimely conclusion by the outbreak of war, laid bare the pattern and footings of the palace buildings, an absorbing exercise, for the excavators had a wealth of documentary guidance.

From the time of William the Conqueror Clarendon Palace had an intermittent royal history. It was a hunting lodge to be enjoyed in time of peace, and times were not always peaceful. War, crusades, interregnums and other commotions interfered with hunting the deer, and at times the palace was left unoccupied for decades on end. Then a strong king with leisure for peaceful pursuits would remember his Wiltshire retreat and send down a commission to report on its condition. Repairs would be ordered, new building decreed, and the palace would enter a new era of glory. Much of the paperwork associated with these visitations has survived, and the archaeologists had an intriguing task trying to match their documents with what they found on the ground.

The palace was finally abandoned during the Wars of the Roses. When Queen Elizabeth I came to hunt in Clarendon Forest, it was too ruinous to be worth repairing and she made do with temporary booths. Bushes and brambles took over, to be replaced in turn by trees. It is the inevitable fate of ancient buildings to be covered by the densest forest that the soil and climate will support. That is because the plough has difficulty in working over masonry footings and foundations.

Almost every suitable square yard of lowland England has been ploughed and exploited for the past three or four thousand years. Modern research has demonstrated that in most places there were no real breaks in occupation between Bronze Age and Iron Age, between Iron Age and Roman estates, between Romans and Saxons, and so to the present day.

The earliest inhabitant of the Pitton valley of whom any trace has been discovered was buried there, in what is now a garden by The Green, in about 1500 BC. He was approximately coeval with the builders of Stonehenge (some ten miles away). On the threshold of historic times men met for festivals and fairs at the nearby enclosure of Figsbury Rings, three miles to the north, and the sunken ways which were the tracks they used are still visible, as are the rectangular 'Celtic' fields on the northern downs overlooking the Pitton valley.

The people who cultivated those fields in Roman times lived in a village, well marked by hummocks and earthworks, on the hill about a mile to the north of the present village. It has never been excavated, but its cemetery has, in the 1950s. The burials were partly inhumations and partly cremations, the ashes being interred in urns. They were grouped around a deep pit, filled with a substance which puzzled the excavators but which Pitton folk declared was disintegrated chalk cob. It seems that the pit may have been in a circular thatched building of chalk cob, the walls of which subsequently collapsed inwards.

Interesting light was thrown on the lives of these early villages. Some had been badly hacked about, though whether before or after death was impossible to say. One youth had been decapitated. The bones of an old woman had been badly crippled by arthritis but, although she was obviously an unproductive member of the community, the family had continued to feed her. The excavators suggested she may well have been regarded as a witch!

Some of the skeletons had been buried in wooden coffins, though with the minimum number of nails required to make each coffin. Some were buried with their boots on, a fact established by the hobnails, the boots having rotted away. But at least they had boots, which suggested to the archaeologists that this was a village of poor but independent peasants, not slaves.

Across a ridge on the opposite side of a downland bottom to their village the Roman road from Old Sarum

(Sorbiodunum) to Winchester (Venta Belgarum) runs in a ruler-straight line. In accordance with Roman custom, these peasants were doubtless held responsible for keeping the road in repair, while their more affluent neighbours on the Roman estates on the better land to the south probably escaped scot-free.

For the heavy clay land which extends to the very edge of the hill that is the southern boundary of the Pitton valley is good farming soil. It links with the Hampshire Basin by way of the Deanbrook, a little stream that has fashioned for itself a shallow valley which eventually leads to the River Test near Romsey. Straddling the Deanbrook valley, about five miles south of Pitton, is the village of West Dean, whose railway station was built on the site of a large and evidently important Roman villa.

Roman villas are best thought of as the headquarters of rural estates, and the West Dean estate seems to have been an extensive one. A mile or so along the valley a much smaller villa was discovered and excavated in the 1920s. It may have held a subsidiary relationship with the Dean villa. Two miles to the north, and situated on the slopes leading up to the Pitton escarpment, is yet another Roman site. It lies in a small wood to the west of the winding lane between Pitton and Farley. Although now almost forgotten, in the period dealt with in this book a side lane, called Nemett's Lane, led to the site. Nemett's Lane! What an evocative name! For in Roman-Britain times *nemeta* was a word used for a shrine, a place sacred to some local deity.

Speculation may perhaps be allowed a little scope here. Was this a place of worship frequented by the labourers or slaves working on the villa estate? Coins of the third and fourth centuries AD have been found on the site. Votive offerings?

And what of the Celtic peasants in their hill-top village? Did they also worship here? A more likely alternative suggests itself. In Celtic lore wells, springs and trees had their resident nymphs and goddesses. On the floor of the Pitton valley Aymers Pond occupies a site in the heart of the village. In what was once a circular enclosure, on a slightly raised plateau adjoining the pond, St Peter's Church stands. Largely rebuilt in the 1880s, it retains some features of the building which was erected in the twelfth century.

Tradition has remarkable tenacity. When, early in the nineteenth century, the village Methodists decided they must have their own place of worship, they felt obliged to build their chapel on a site as near as possible to the church. No more than a few yards separated the two buildings. In an earlier age, did Christian converts pay heed to Pope Gregory's instructions? 'The idol temples are not to be destroyed, but let the idols in them be destroyed; let holy water be blessed and and sprinkled in these temples, let altars be built and relics placed there; and since they are accustomed to slay many oxen in sacrifice to demons, let them on the anniversary of the dedication, or on the birthdays of the holy martyrs, construct booths around those churches which were formerly temples, and celebrate the solemnity with religious festivity.'

It seems at least feasible. From their hilltop perch the inhabitants of Pitton's predecessor may well have made regular visits to pay their respects to the spirit of the pool.

The pond is, in fact, in wet winters the headwaters of a winterbourne (see pp.114-16) which farther down becomes the Deanbrook, and springs rise from its floor. Bearing in mind that in some parts of the Wessex chalk country the water table is said to have fallen by as much as 150 feet since the Roman era, Pitton could have had a permanent stream in those days.

The career of the hill-top village seems to have ended in the last few decades of the fourth century AD. The latest coins recovered from the graveyard, where some were placed in the mouths of the deceased (presumably to pay the ferryman to transport their souls across the Styx), belong to the period of the Emperors Constantinus and Constantius around AD 340-60. The latest coins found at the *nemeta* are of approximately the same period.

It fits in with known history. In the year 367 the tide of barbarians which had been a growing menace to Roman civilization in Britain throughout the century burst through the barriers and poured over the land in a devastating flood. Plundering and murdering gangs roamed at will over the countryside, indulging in an orgy of destruction. Fortified towns were bypassed, but villas were easy prey. It was probably during this holocaust that the villas in the Deanbrook valley and the peasant village on the hill disappeared. A mob moving along the great road linking Winchester and Sarum could have fanned out and wrought havoc to their hearts' content. One can conjecture that many disaffected slaves would have joined them.

For the next 700 years the history of the valley is a virtual blank. A single reference in the ninth century to Pitan-werth is thought to refer to Pitton. The name is apparently derived from the Anglo-Saxon personal name Pitta or Putta – the hawk. It could have belonged to the leader who founded a new village in the valley, by the pool, or it could imply that this was the place where Anglo-Saxon nobles kept their hawks. Possible support for the latter theory is that throughout the Middle Ages Pitton was a forest village, with close associations with Clarendon Palace. In the present century a carved arrowhead, of the sort used in hunting rather than in war, was dug up in a Pitton garden. Perhaps this is where the royal hawks were kept.

The omission of Pitton from the Domesday Book is curious but fits in logically with the subsequent history of the village. Until 1874 Pitton was reckoned a chapelry of the parish of Alderbury, four miles to the south. In 1874 it was linked with Farley to create a new parish – Pitton and Farley.

At Alderbury, on the edge of Clarendon Park, stood the priory of Ivychurch. Throughout the Middle Ages this priory was the residence of a prior and thirteen canons. Their prime duty was to minister to the spiritual needs of the King and his Court when they were in residence at Clarendon. Subsidiary were the religious affairs of the forest settlements, which included Pitton and the other chapelries.

As a royal park, Clarendon was ex-parochial. Salisbury Cathedral was considered its parish church. Also it did not feature in the standard taxation rolls. That presumably is the reason for the omission of the forest settlements from the Domesday Book, which was primarily a record compiled for the purposes of taxation.

Apart from its anomalous status as a detached part of a somewhat distant parish, the only apparent associations of Pitton with the Ivychurch priory are two place-names, Abbots' Close and Monkey's Castle. The first refers to a close opposite the church and linking the High Street with The Green, but the prior of Ivychurch was not an abbot, and the name may refer to a later character named Abbott. Monkey's Castle may have originally been Monke's Castle but, on the other hand, it may simply be a fanciful name, perhaps given by children, to a yew wood clinging to a steep cliff by White Hill.

One other echo of medieval times lingers at Pitton. Throughout the Middle Ages the Roman road between Sarum and Winchester remained an important highway. As it approaches the present London road (A30), the lane from Pitton crosses it on the crest of a steep hill – Joyner's Hill. A hundred yards to the east a track leaves the Roman road and follows the scarp for several miles, direct to the site of Clarendon Palace. During the medieval centuries the track (though it may have been no more than a broad band of hoofmarks over open downland) must have been in frequent use.

In the 1920s almost every Pitton villager knew the story of ghostly horsemen, whom some professed to have seen, riding along the crest of Joyner's Hill. Generally they were alleged to have been seen on winter evenings by passengers returning from Salisbury by carrier's cart. Surely a remarkable instance of folk-memory!

Charles II on his Restoration to the throne in 1660 gave the Clarendon estate to George Monke, Duke of Albemarle. Over the next fifty years it changed hands several times and in 1713 was purchased by a Mr Benjamin Bathurst, whose descendants continued to own it until 1919. Sir

Frederick Bathurst at Clarendon was an important part of the background to life in Pitton in the first two decades of the present century, to be succeeded briefly by the Gartons and then by the Christie-Miller family, who still own the estate.

In the seventeenth century, however, a new noble family appeared on the scene and exercised considerable dominance for near on 200 years.

Early in that century a clever boy of Farley secured a good education at Salisbury Cathedral School. Later, seeking his fortune in London, Stephen Fox became attached to the household of the dukes of Northumberland. During the Civil War he naturally found himself on the Royalist side. It is said that, when fleeing from the Battle of Worcester in 1651, Charles II hid briefly at Farley, including taking refuge in a ditch! When he went into exile on the Continent, Stephen Fox went with him and proved to be a financial genius, contriving somehow to keep the royal household functioning when money was almost non-existent.

On his Restoration Charles rewarded his faithful servant by making him Paymaster of the Forces. After the fashion of that time Stephen took care to pay himself for all the deprivations he had suffered, thus laying the foundations of a very considerable fortune.

Sir Richard Colt Hoare, the Wiltshire historian and antiquarian, relates that in his old age Stephen was a frustrated and disappointed man. His ambition was to found a family of landed gentry, and he had the necessary money, but he had only one son who, now in his fifties, had failed to produce an heir and seemed unlikely to do so. So, when past his eightieth year, Stephen decided that, if his son declined to do his duty, he himself had better take a hand. He found a suitable heiress from Lincolnshire and proposed marriage. She was at first taken aback at being courted by this old man but on reflection accepted, doubtless taking into consideration that he was unlikely to last long. Possibly to her surprise, within the next four years she gave birth to four children, including twin boys. Soon afterwards the old man died happy.

His dynasty proved every bit as illustrious as Stephen Fox could have hoped, for the Fox family dominated English politics for much of the eighteenth and early nineteenth centuries. One of the twins became the first Earl of Holland, the other the first Earl of Ilchester.

For their landed estates, these two went back to their ancestral home. The Earl of Ilchester acquired the manors of Farley and Pitton, the Earl of Holland the manor of the neighbouring village of Winterslow. For both, however, these manors were only parts of their possessions. The earls of Ilchester purchased vast estates in Dorset and Somerset, making their home at Melbury. The earls of Holland gained possession of many hundreds of acres on the western outskirts of London – the Mayfair estate, then open country.

The second Earl of Holland determined to make his family seat at Winterslow and caused a magnificent mansion to be built there. Soon after its completion it was burnt down. The Earl tried again but in 1774, as a ball was being held to celebrate its opening, another fire started and again the result was total destruction. This time the disheartened Earl abandoned Winterslow and concentrated instead on his London estates – a fortunate decision for his successors.

There are few visible reminders now of the association of the Hollands with Winterslow, except for two large cedar trees in a meadow which was once the home park. Some intriguing place-names, though, are still in everyday use. There is, for instance, a cottage called Pimlico and a clump of trees called Soho. And the hilltop clump of beeches that looks down on Pitton from the north is Piccadilly Clump.

The Ilchester family remained associated with Pitton and Farley much longer. The earls of Ilchester retained the lands as a sporting estate, travelling up from their Dorset home at intervals during winter for a day's shooting. Records still exist of their bags (consisting mainly of pheasants, partridges and hares but also an occasional woodcock). They did not finally part with the estate until 1912, an event which is the chief reason for taking that date as the base-line for this book. Until then Pitton and Farley were villages of tenant farmers on a sporting estate. In 1912 they gained their final independence.

Throughout the nineteenth century the estate was managed for the Earl by agents who were the biggest farmers and who usually resided at Farley. The last of the line was Emanuel Parsons, an efficient and energetic farmer who was evidently well liked and respected. But for the villagers it was not quite the same as having a resident squire keeping a constant eye on them. The Bathursts at Clarendon Palace loomed larger in the lives of the people of Pitton than did the Ilchesters of Melbury.

To emphasize further their independence, the Pitton villagers had no resident parson either. For a time in the nineteenth century a curate had been appointed from Alderbury, and a house, Church House, was built for him. But when the new parish of Pitton and Farley was created, the vicar took up residence at Farley, largely because a suitable house was available there. Stephen Fox had caused a splendid new church to be built at Farley. It has often been described as Wren Church, Stephen and Sir Christopher Wren being old friends, but the accepted opinion seems to be that the church is the work of one of Wren's understudies. Opposite the new church is a handsome block of almshouses, flanking an imposing brick residence, the Wardenry. Its purpose was to provide a house for the warden of the almshouses, an arrangement which for years was happily construed as providing a vicarage, the vicar automatically holding the post of warden. (Within recent years the arrangement has been altered.)

When the estate came up for sale, the village farmers and householders were naturally much exercised about their future. Those who could afford to bought their holdings. Many cottagers who felt such a venture beyond their means arranged for neighbours to buy the property and retain them as tenants. The Parsons family helped out a number of them in this way.

Among the farming tenants were six who were in the process of improving their lot in life. Hearing of the 1910

Smallholdings Act, they approached the Wiltshire Country Council with the request that part of the estate should be purchased and let out to them as tenant smallholders. The County Council agreed, and the transaction was concluded satisfactorily. The little farms were larger than the normal size of smallholdings but that was deemed acceptable on such poor chalk soil as the fields by Bottom Way.

2 *The Farms and the Farmers*

The 1851 census for Pitton catalogues nine farmers. By 1912 the number had risen to eleven. But it all depends on what one means by a farmer. Even in 1851 George Cooke is classified as a farmer, though there is added in parenthesis 'of six acres'.

1819 was the year of Pitton's main Enclosure Act. There had evidently been an earlier one, for the Award Map shows the fields on the southern side of the village labelled 'Ancient Enclosures'. The part of the village lands dealt with by the 1819 Parliamentary Act consisted of the fields, then probably one large field, along the valley north of the village. Doubtless it was managed according to the

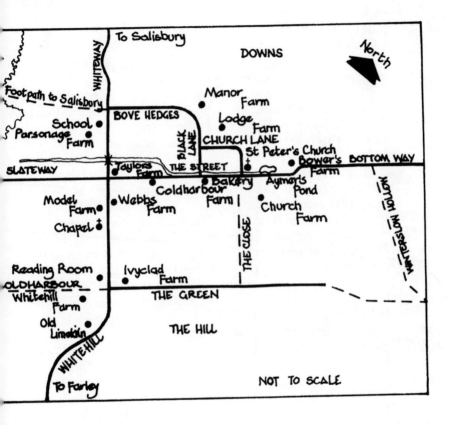

old open-field system, whereby it was divided into strips, normally 220 yards (one furlong) long by 22 yards (one chain) wide, producing a measurement of one acre. The general rule was that no farmer or peasant should have two contiguous strips, thus preventing one man's acquiring all the best land. And to make the system even fairer, all the strips were re-allocated each year, in some instances by ballot.

Another provision was that the great field should be devoted entirely to the same crop. Thus when the crop was wheat, everybody had to grow wheat. Next year it would probably be barley. In the third year the land would be fallowed, in preparation for wheat again.

How this rotation worked out for Pitton is not easy to see. Usually there were as many great fields as there were alternative crops, so that in each year there would be two fields devoted to crops and one fallow. Pitton would seem to have had only one great field in the years immediately before 1819. Or perhaps the valley fields were divided into two or three main sections before being subdivided into strips.

When the fields on the other (southern) side of the village were enclosed is unknown, but the adjective 'ancient' is probably used accurately. Though now parcelled into no more than three farms, they were, within living memory, divided into small fields of about an acre. Indeed, the arrangement was very like that of the strips in the open great field, except that each field was in the permanent possession of one farmer. Most of the village farmers, however, had a field or two on this southern side and other fields on the open country on the northern side.

Again this seems to have been a fair arrangement, for it gave each village farmer some light chalk soil and some heavy clay soil. The little fields on the southern side possessed another very considerable asset: each had boundary hedges almost as wide as the field itself, and these hedges abounded in hazel, ash, maple, holly, oak and other useful timber where a man could cut fencing posts, rods for hurdles and thatching spars, faggots for burning, logs, tool handles and all the other manifold items that could be made from underwood. The hedges were, in fact, not so much hedges as survivals of the primitive forest which once clothed the clay country. In spring they were alive with primroses, bluebells, wood anemones and bird song.

One sound economic reason for the Enclosure Acts, heavily though they bore on the poorer cottagers, was that they opened the way for technical improvements in agriculture. Before that, under the open-field system, there was no incentive for a man to improve his soil, knowing that next year he would be cultivating different strips.

The other handicap in the old system was the waste of time spent in moving from one strip to another. Curiously, that aspect of the old way of life was perpetuated in Pitton to the very end of the period under review – 1939.

It can be seen in its extreme in the story of old Elisha Whitlock, who lived in the last decades of the nineteenth century. His house, like that of so many of his Pitton contemporaries, was a cottage in a close, or paddock, somewhere in the High Street, probably in Sinnett's Close. The back door gave directly onto a muddy yard flanked by a ramshackle collection of sheds and lean-tos, and to reach them the old man had to negotiate an obstacle course of dungheaps. The buildings were a patchwork of rough timber and hurdlework, with roofs thatched by the inexpert hands of Elisha himself, this being before the age of galvanized iron.

Buildings and yard were populated by three cows, a dozen or so hens, an almost equal number of cockerels, three geese, a pig, several cats and a mongrel dog. The cows' progeny, of various ages, wandered about in the paddock beyond, in the shade of four decrepit apple trees. At one side of the house was Elisha's vegetable garden, in the corner of which, under an ancient yew, stood a stack of wood faggots and the shed where he kept his tools. Under the deep eaves of the cottage, where the roof began only three feet above ground, several bee-skeps sat on a wooden bench which once a year served as a pig-killing stool.

Now, theoretically and probably in his own opinion, Elisha could be classified as a farmer, for, in addition to the yard and paddock, which comprised something less than an acre, he possessed two little fields. They were situated in a corner of land where Dunley Hill joins Cockroad. Their total was not more than four acres, of which nearly half was taken up by broad hazel hedges. Elisha did not cultivate these little fields; they were meadow land.

On rising in the morning, Elisha fed the calves, cows and pig and milked the cows. Then, after a leisurely breakfast, he proceeded to drive the cows to pasture. A glance at the map on p.29 will show that this was a considerable journey. The little herd wandered up the village street and along the lane marked 'Slate Way'. This lane had broad, grassy margins on which the cows could graze. Elisha did not hurry them. The roadside grazing was an essential part of his economy. If along the way anyone had thoughtlessly left a gate open, the cows naturally wandered in and helped themselves to whatever was growing there. If someone happened to spot them, they would be sure to see Elisha also, working himself up into a proper frenzy as he noisily endeavoured to turn them out; but if no one was about, he let them take their fill.

By the time the cows arrived at their pasture it was past eleven o'clock. Elisha leaned over the gate, enjoying his pipe, or cut a bit of hazel if he felt like it. There were snares to be inspected both in the hedges around the fields and in the neighbourhood roadside hedges. At mid-day he strolled back home to dinner ('nammit', as he called it).

At two o'clock it was time to go and fetch the cows home for milking. Again the leisurely stroll, allowing time for a gossip with anyone who happened to be available, the setting of snares in places which his experienced eyes suggested as promising, and, of course, an hour or two's grazing for the cows. So the days pursued their comfortable pattern.

In summer Elisha was available to help with haymaking and harvest for his bigger neighbours. Sometimes he contracted to do a bit of hoeing. With his scythe he mowed grass verges to roadsides which nobody else claimed. In autumn he gathered hazel-nuts. If he felt energetic enough, he sometimes bought the standing underwood in a section of forest and joined the woodmen. But it was against his principles to do anything too energetic or exacting. He managed very well, thank you, without exerting himself overmuch.

In essence Elisha's was a straightforward adaptation of the traditional way of life of English commoners for many centuries. Under the open-field system which prevailed throughout the Middle Ages the great grain fields with

Annie Pearce at Pond Cottage, *c.*1920. Note seed-boxes on window-sill

Ralph Whitlock at White Hill Farm, *c.*1924. Note his white collar and bow tie!

Ralph (leaning against the gate) with his father Ted at Webb's Farm

Ralph's mother outside White Hill Farm before the west wing was added in 1921. Note the rustic frame—the pig rack where carcases were hung for dismembering. Ted Whitlock was the village pig-killer. The hedge is largely of hop-vines

A good turnout for the chapel Sunday school outing to Amesbury, *c.*1913

Riding in the charabanc for the church Sunday school outing, *c.*1932

White dresses for the Sunday school festival, *c.*1939. In the background lie the buildings and farmhouse of Model Farm

Pitton chapel celebrates the opening of the new Sunday school, 1938

The village street with the 'springs' in full flood

John Webb's funeral, 1920

Pitton School in about 1915 with their teacher Miss Packer. Note the pinafores and buttoned boots

Pitton School in 1919

The author wearing his grandfather's smock and carrying his father's crook

their individual strips were complemented by a large area of common land. This was not land belonging to the general public, as is sometimes thought nowadays, but land belonging to the community. It was shared between members of the community according to well-defined rights.

A peasant would be entitled to a stated number of strips in each of the cultivated fields and also certain rights on the common. 'Pasturage' conferred the right to turn a stated number of grazing animals, generally cattle, to graze there. 'Pannage' was the right to turn pigs loose in the forest, where they could get much of their living by grubbing out roots and, in autumn, by eating acorns and beech-mast. Right of turbary entitled the peasant to cut turf or dig peat. 'Estovers' was the right to gather wood (from uprooted trees) and 'wyndfallen' wood (from branches blown off trees by the wind). There were also rights covering geese on the common. Parish officials, known as agisters, were appointed to ensure that no one exceeded his statutory common rights.

So it can be imagined that the medieval peasant would, like Elisha Whitlock, spent much of his time plodding from strip to strip in the arable fields or taking his livestock to graze on the common. Elisha was doing, under somewhat changed circumstances, more or less what his ancestors had done for untold generations. One of the complaints made by the aristocracy when trying to justify the enclosures was that the peasant was an idle layabout anyway. In their view he was a member of what they termed the labouring classes, and they maintained that he never put in a full day's labour. One can see their point, though it is fair to add that the most vociferous critics never did a day's work in their lives.

There is no record of Pitton's ever possessing a common, though tradition has it that the back lane now known as The Green was once the village green and was at least thirty yards wide for its entire length. The pattern followed by Elisha Whitlock continued, to a certain extent, long after his death and that out of necessity.

Pitton is a compact village, its farms and cottages

grouped around the church. One reason for this seems to have been the water supply. Not only were the ponds, of which Aymer's Pond was the chief, naturally situated in the lowest part of the valley but the wells on which the villagers had to rely in summer were also shallowest there. In the 1920s and 1930s the wells along the High Street were in general about eighty feet deep but that of White Hill Farm was 120 feet. With every bucket of water having to be drawn up by windlass, depth was a consideration.

The general arrangement, therefore, was for each farm to be provided with a house, buildings, yard and back paddock in the village proper. Before enclosure it would then cultivate so many acres in the open fields and possess certain common rights. When the 'ancient enclosures' occurred, most of the farmers acquired one or more of the little fields which were carved out of what may then have been common land. When the 1819 enclosures happened, the same arrangement was made. So, in the 1920s a typical Pitton farm consisted of a house, farmyard and one meadow in the village, together with several small fields with broad hedges on the clay soil of the southern hill and a larger acreage of open arable land by Bottom Way.

Under the old style of farming this arrangement posed no real problems, for the traditional pattern on the chalk lands of southern England was based on sheep and corn. The sheep were hurdle flocks, feeding on the downs in summer but on crops specially grown for them, chiefly turnips, on the arable fields in winter. Their droppings during the winter months manured the soil, causing the sheep to be referred to as 'the golden hoof'.

The bottom dropped out of this time-honoured rural economy when cargoes of grain and refrigerated meat started to arrive in Britain, beginning in 1875. Thereafter the now predominantly urban populace relied for its food on cheap imports, and British agriculture sank into a prolonged depression. Corn crops were hardly worth growing, and keeping sheep was a sure way of losing money. Those who persisted in sticking to the traditional rotation were weeded out by bankruptcies.

But what to replace the sheep? The answer had to be cows. The market for meat and wheat had apparently disappeared but milk trains still ran daily from Salisbury to London. One of the first commercial motor vehicles the village acquired was a lorry to take churns of milk from the local farms to the Salisbury depot. Pitton was on the way to becoming a village of dairymen.

It was a role to which it was not naturally suited. The improvising farmers had no tradition, such as existed in parts of Dorset, Somerset and other counties, of taking the bucket and stool to the pasture and milking the cows there. In any case, there was no water in the fields, so the cows had to come home to drink. So, as with Elisha's little herd, the Pitton cows went out to the fields after the morning milking and returned for the evening milking. It was a poor arrangement, for they had no access to water during the day, when they were making milk, but the farmers knew no alternative. Sometimes in summer the herds went back to the fields for the night, but mostly they stayed tied in their stalls or idling in the back paddock.

Four of the herds made their daily pilgrimage along Bottom Way, and some thought had to be given to timing or battles ensued. In a herd a pecking order is soon established and is known and respected by all the members, but cows will always fight with those of another herd. Often the four herds could be seen meandering homewards at the same time, a well-calculated space between each herd. And care had to be taken not to hurry them, so that each in turn could be allowed time to drink at the foul waters of Aymer's Pond. Ted Whitlock's problem was a particularly tricky one, for he had to negotiate the final section High Street, where there was the possible hazard of encountering Jack Judd's cows emerging from Slate Way on their way home to Cold Harbour Farm.

The time has come to introduce the Pitton farmers of the period 1912-39. First, the lucky ones, who had farms within a ring fence, enabling them to operate without taking their cows on the road.

Manor Farm, occupying the best site in the village, on a southward sloping hill with the sun shining on it all day, was the domain of Mr Ted Judd. He is remembered as a quiet, unassuming man who remained rather aloof from village life. Manor Farm fell to his lot because that is where he was living at the time of the Sale, and there seemed no reason for him to move when that part of the estate was purchased by the County Council Smallholdings Committee. His fields ran from his house – a fine but somewhat dilapidated one of Queen Anne or Georgian date – north to the Winterbourne parish boundary and west to Whiteway.

On the opposite side of Whiteway, Parsonage Farm fitted in between the road and the Clarendon estate. Its southern boundary was Slateway. The Clarendon property here was mostly woodland, its boundary marked by a deep ditch and flanking bank known as 'the Deer Leap' – a feature doubtless of medieval origin and intended to keep the royal deer from straying. Parsonage Farmhouse was a three-storeyed brick-and-tile building, of probably about the same date as Manor Farm. Both farms were well equipped with substantial buildings and spacious home paddocks.

At the beginning of the period the farm tenant was a Mr Reg Hawkins, who is now barely remembered locally. At the Sale, however, or soon afterwards it was acquired by a Mr Penn, a baker and shopkeeper of Grimstead. His daughter married Owen Griffin, who from the time he returned from the 1914-18 war, during much of which he was prisoner-of-war, played a leading part in local affairs. He represented the village for many years on the Salisbury District Council, of which he was in due course Chairman for a time, and he was also on the councils of the local branch of the National Farmers Union and other organizations. A slim, handsome man of rather above medium height, he was well educated and an excellent public speaker, but during those years of agricultural depression the economic dice were loaded against him and he was probably denied the rewards he deserved.

The third ring-fence farm was Lodge Farm, its house

tucked in at the corner of Black Lane and Church Lane, and its land extending a field or two wide alongside Manor Farm. The old thatched farmhouse and buildings had been burnt down around the time of the Sale and were replaced by a modern red-brick and slate house. Here for the early part of the period lived Mr Uriah Whitlock, almost invariably referred to as Toby Whitlock, for there was another Uriah Whitlock who kept the village shop. A childless couple, he and his wife lived a quiet life, and the village saw little of them, though one gathers that it had not always been so.

The fourth ring-fence farm occupied the next rectangular section of the estate acquired by the Smallholdings Committee, sharing a boundary with Lodge Farm. Its north-eastern boundary was the muddy lane known as 'The Drove'. Its farmhouse was small, not bigger than the average cottage, and was tucked away with its farmyard behind the top end of Aymer's Pond. Bower's Farm was its name, and its tenant was Stephen Seaward. Stephen was an old man at the time of the Sale and had been in residence for many years. He claimed to be the fifth generation of Seawards farming those fields, and the parish register testifies to the presence of Seawards in the village for the previous two centuries. Yet the fact that the farm was known as Bower's Farm implies an earlier tenant of that name.

There was a fifth ring-fence farm, of very recent origin. This was the outlying Bentley Farm, fitted against the Winterslow parish boundary on the south side of Bottom Way. It had been carved out of the Pitton open fields at some time early in the present century and was now occupied by Mr Lionel Seaward, Stephen Seaward's son. During the years of depression he suffered like the rest and was not noted for the excellence of his crops but, being childless, like Toby Whitlock, he got by.

Jack Judd came near to being a ring-fence farmer, all his fields but one lying within a ring-fence on the south side of Slateway. Dunley Hill was their south-western boundary, and they were transected by Cockroad, but that had no practical disadvantage, for no other Pitton farmer had land down that lane. The field that lay outside the ring-fence, however, was the paddock at the back of the farmhouse and farmstead, in the middle of the village. So, like other Pitton farmers, Jack Judd had to take his cows along a section of highway between his main pastures and his milking shed. His house was a typical thatched farmhouse, of medium size, the yard being flanked by a range of thatched buildings.

Jack was the younger brother of Ted Judd of Manor Farm. Their father was old Stephen Judd, who had come from Broadchalke or Bishopstone to take the tenancy of a Pitton farm in the 1890s. At the beginning of the period he was living with his son Jack at Cold Harbour Farm and is remembered as a handsome old man, with a benign face and magnificent white side-whiskers. The village children were greatly afraid of him, for in June he laid in wait for them on a piece of shrub land just beyond Cockroad and chased them with a stick when they came to pick wild strawberries.

At the corner in the centre of the village, Taylor's Farm was occupied by Tom Collins and his son Sam. Tom, a chubby, round man, was a cripple, swinging himself along with the help of two crutches. (It was said that his injuries resulted from his being dropped as a baby.) His farm consisted of a paddock at the rear of his farmhouse, a yard with stables, barn and other buildings on the opposite side of the village street, and a collection of fields along Bottom Way. These comprised a field known as Old Lawn, at the junction of Bottom Way and Winterslow Hollow, another known as Stony Lawn, and a square of land at the top end of The Drove.

Tom was also one of the two village carriers driving to Salisbury on Tuesdays and Saturdays. Between times he did a bit of hauling of faggots and other underwood products, leaving most of the farm work to his unmarried son, Sam. Another son, Walter, owned a steam threshing-machine with which he did contract work. Early in the 1920s Walter and his family emigrated – to Norfolk. The entire village assembled to wave farewell to them as they sat on piles of furniture on an iron-wheeled waggon hitched behind the threshing tackle. They made the journey at walking pace and were never seen in Pitton again.

The Collins farm seems to have been a synthetic one, of fields with no tradition of being worked together, and the house itself had, not long before the Sale, been two cottages. The farmhouse associated with the barns and other farm buildings had, in fact, been at one time Lavender Cottage. This is an interesting example of a farmhouse and cottages changing status, the farmhouse becoming a cottage and the two cottages being made to serve as the farmhouse.

At the end of the Street, opposite the church and Aymers Pond, Church Farm stood on a slight eminence well back from the road and approached by way of a footpath across a paddock. Behind it a paddock gave access to The Green, so it was possible for the farm cows to reach some of the fields without traversing the Bottom Way. But the main block of the farm's land lay on the north side of Bottom Way, half a mile from the village, so the cows were normally one of the herds that trod the familiar track and drank at Aymer's Pond.

Church Farm's farmer was Luther White, whose father had lived there before him. Joshua White, however, was one of those peasant farmers who had rented a few fields from the Earl of Ilchester and gained much of his living by dealing. When his family was young, he used to walk the six miles each way to Wallop to collect eggs and butter and get back to Pitton in time to catch the carrier's cart which left for Salisbury at eight o'clock.

In addition to his main block of fields by Bottom Way Luther had two or three smaller ones, between the village and Winterslow Hollow, a section of hillside above them, and some clay-land fields over the crest of the hill. Church Farm itself is a thatched house of moderate size, overlooking a quite spacious farmyard with the usual complement of buildings.

Luther's elder brother Lewis occupied the group of rectangular fields on the north of The Drove and the block of hill land rising up to Piccadilly Clump. On the north side it marched with the hedge that was the boundary of Luther's land. Lewis lived in a little farmhouse called Model Farm, not far from the foot of White Hill and on the south side of the road. Behind it he possessed a small range of buildings and two small paddocks.

The name 'Model Farm' is interesting because it bears evidence of having been originally planned as a model farm, perhaps as far back as Tudor times. The farmhouse was small but compact and was equipped with an adequate kitchen and dairy. Perched on a bank on the edge of the road, it drew its water supply from a well outside the front door. A wide, brick-paved path along the rear of the buildings, protected by thatched eaves, led to a well-planned range of stables, cowsheds and barns. The demolition of this intriguing antique, in the 1950s or '60s, was a tragic loss.

Lewis followed the family tradition of dealing and was also one of the two village carriers, making his journey to Salisbury in his old black-tilted waggon on Tuesdays and Saturdays. Those still living who have travelled with him remember that the journey took about 2½ hours and that coming up the hills when homeward bound they often had to get out and push.

Ted Whitlock was probably the least favoured of the Pitton farmers in that he didn't even possess a farmyard. He lived in a two-bedroomed cottage at the foot of White Hill, at the corner of The Green and Cold Harbour, the land attached to it being less than a quarter of an acre. Perched on a bank looking westward over the valley, it was approached by way of a sloping path at the foot of which stood two derelict cottages, a thatched barn and a stable. These were adapted by Ted as his farm buildings. He later added to them a cowshed, hay-store and garage, and at about the same time – in the early 1920s – he also built a new wing to his cottage, transforming it into a pleasant four-bedroomed house.

He was, however, still handicapped by having no fields nearby and, to make matters worse, his was the section of Smallholdings Committee land farthest along Bottom Way, a good mile from the village. This was not such a serious handicap in the days when the allocation of land was made and farming was based on sheep, but it became a severe disadvantage when the sheep were of necessity superseded by cows.

Like most of the other village farmers, Ted came from peasant stock, his immediate forebears being agricultural labourers. Unlucky in the death of his father when Ted was a baby of six months, he used often to relate how his widowed mother reared a family of three children on the pauper's payment of five shillings a week and two loaves of workhouse bread. Marrying a daughter of Joshua White, he began to acquire a little land as a tenant of the Earl of Ilchester and before the Sale was cultivating twelve acres by Cockroad. Unfortunately for him, he lost this at the Sale and had to negotiate with the Smallholdings Committee instead.

On the opposite side of White Hill to Model Farm, Webb's Farm was the home of William Clark. Like so many of the other Pitton farmers, William had a small, compact farmhouse and farmyard and a back paddock. He also had a further paddock of about an acre on the other side of the road, significantly known as Club Close, of which more later. He differed from most of the other farmers, however, in that most of his fields were situated on the farther side of the hill. To get to them demanded a long, wearying climb up a gradient of one in nine. Once there, the fields, comprising about forty-five acres, were more fertile than the valley farms, being on heavy clay. Consisting of land which in the 1819 map had been classified as 'Ancient Enclosures', each field was bounded by wide hazel hedges, regarded as a considerable asset and much utilized.

Will Clark had been trained as a carpenter and builder and still worked at times for one of the local building firms. He must have realized when farming fell into such doldrums that cows offered the only way of salvation, for he was on very difficult ground, with that formidable hill between his farmstead and his fields. In about 1924 he sold his farm, which was bought by a local landowner, Mr Knapman, and let to Ted Whitlock, for whom fields somewhat nearer home were a godsend.

The imposing scarp shadowing the village and providing such a splendid panorama of the valley belonged to the farm of Mr Reg Eyres, who lived at Ivyclad Farm at the foot of the hill. His land consisted of the hill and a block of three fields on the far side, a farmhouse and set of buildings at the junction of White Hill and The Green. At some time within the period under consideration he was also farming a largish block of upland fields in Winterbourne parish, on the road to Salisbury, though in that era of depression and dereliction much of the land was often unploughed.

Reg was an elderly, heavily built, bald man, mild in manner and not over-energetic. He came from a family who originated in Alderbury, where their ancestor was a tollgate keeper. They probably had connections with the builder of that notable landmark on Whiteparish Hill, the Pepperbox, more properly known as Eyre's Folly, and with the Eyres family who still hold important positions in and around the New Forest.

In Pitton the Eyres also ran a builders' business, which they had taken over when the Brieants went bankrupt. In the 1915 Post Office Directory they are entered as 'Eyres & Sons, Wheelwrights'. The head of the firm then was old Edward Eyres, Reg's father. In front of the farmhouse, ranges of timber buildings, which formed two sides of a quadrangle, were occupied mainly by the carpenters and waggon-builders. Edward Eyres had an off-licence to sell beer at Ivyclad Farm, and another of his sons, Archie, kept the Pheasant Inn on the London road, then known as Winterslow Hut.

In a cob-walled, slate-roofed cottage under the hill lived Lot Whitlock, his wife and three children. Lot had a little farm of curious composition though very similar basically to most of the Pitton farms. It consisted of a small farmyard with sheds and paddocks on the opposite side of The Green, a rectangle of fields on the east side of Bottom Way, and two small fields by the lane halfway to Farley.

In a somewhat dilapidated, cob-walled thatched cottage tucked in below the carpenters' sheds lived Edward Shellum and his family. At the beginning of the period it was a farmworker's cottage occupied by a family named Lane, but at some time in the 1920s the Shellums arrived, some said from Ireland, some from Wales. Edward Shellum bought, for a derisory sum, a section of downland in Winterbourne parish at the top of Whiteway, on the opposite side of the road to that occupied by Reg Eyres. From this long-derelict land he strove to obtain a living. His property included the site of the Romano-British village, and he found the easiest way to make a set of buildings was to dig into the ancient earthworks and roof the excavation with galvanized iron. Thither he made his way every morning, returning at nightfall and spending the intervening hours cultivating the more promising corners of his hilly domain and attending to the needs of a few cattle. He managed to get by, however, primarily by selling downland turf to Salisbury gardeners.

Such were the farmers whose holdings were the mainstay of the village economy in the two decades between the wars. All but two, namely Owen Griffin and Edward Shellum, were, so to speak, on their home ground. They came from the old peasant stock of the village, or at least from similar stock in neighbouring villages, and most of their families were on the parish register in the early seventeenth century.

The men who acquired their little farms in 1912 were aware that farming was not as it used to be. The older men could remember the halcyon days that faded out in the late 1870s. Until then British agriculture had, by the very efficient system that became known as 'Victorian high farming', just about managed to keep pace with the ever-increasing needs of the urban populace.

The situation throughout that period had been epitomized by pessimistic Malthus who, writing in 1798, postulated that, 'Human kind have a natural tendency to increase beyond the means of sustenance for them.' And for the best part of a century it seemed likely that he was right. The industrialization of Britain forged ahead at an unparalleled rate, and the upsurge of population kept pace with it. Every bit of food the home fields could produce was needed, and still the number of mouths to be fed increased. By about 1870 it seemed that the limit had nearly been reached, and thoughtful observers worried about catastrophe ahead. Then, apparently in the nick of time, food started to arrive from new lands overseas. The prairies of the USA and Canada had been ploughed and were beginning to produce a vast surplus of grain. The technique of sending cargoes of refrigerated meat across the oceans had been perfected, thus opening up the grasslands of Australia, New Zealand, South Africa and South America as larders for the nation.

1875, the watershed year when the shipments started to arrive, heralded disaster for British agriculture. Over the next twenty years prices of farm produce were approximately halved. The price of wheat, for instance, fell from 58s 3d per quarter in 1873 to 26s 2d per quarter in 1896, that of barley from 40s 5d per quarter to 22s 11d. The natural consequence was that the acreage devoted to those crops drastically declined, for grain crops in general by about twenty-five per cent in those twenty years.

It was, of course, the marginal land that was abandoned first, and that included the chalk downlands, large acreages of which had been laboriously brought into cultivation in the years of prosperity. They included most of the downs to the north of Pitton. In the 1920s the villagers were aware of them as miles of dereliction, just over the horizon. It was possible to see the outlines of the deserted fields and even of the plough rudges, for they had been abandoned without even being sown to grass. On some the dominant vegetation was not even weeds but brown and grey lichen. By 1912 the blight had crept over the parish boundary into the top end of the Bottom Way fields, which in the 1920s lay generally uncultivated.

1875-93 were the worst years. Thousands of efficient farmers, trying to carry on farming in the well-tried tradition, went bankrupt. Landowners, despairing of finding tenants for their neglected acres, jettisoned vast areas of farmland as being a liability rather than an asset. They drew in their horns and waited for better times. The Earl of Ilchester was a late disciple of the trend.

As for the purchasers of the estate, they were the slaves

of the immemorial peasant instinct to acquire land. For uncounted generations land had represented food, a livelihood and, above all, security and independence. The Sale of 1912 represented the opportunity of a lifetime.

Whether any of the farmers thus established in 1912 had much appreciation of the background to the changes that were engulfing them is doubtful. Whether they had a full understanding of what was happening may be equally so. For the present they rejoiced at the sequence of events which made their new independence possible.

For the present, too, they had some justification for optimism. Since the 1890s things had marginally improved in agriculture. While there was no general recovery, the bankruptcy flood had been ebbing. The new purchasing power of the cities was becoming interested in fresh farm produce. The Boer War had alerted a Government to defence needs, which tended to take manpower for the services and for armaments.

The general effect was that, when the First World War came, farming was not in too bad shape, though at Pitton the changes had occurred so recently that the new farmers were not really geared to take full advantage of the situation. Their problems were aggravated, of course, by the Government's calling up men indiscriminately for the armed services, with little regard for their normal occupation. It took the nearly successful U-boat campaign to force home the realization that starvation was a real possibility and that men working on the land could do as much for their country as those in the army. As it was, women stepped into the gap and pitched into farmwork.

During the war a million acres of previously derelict land in Britain were reclaimed for wheat-growing, and rather more than that for growing oats for the ubiquitous and all-important horses. Cattle, sheep and poultry greatly increased in numbers. And in 1918 an apparently grateful Government passed a Corn Production Act to protect farmers from the overseas competition that had proved so ruinous over the previous decades. General euphoria prevailed. There was to be no more war, and prosperity was guaranteed.

3 The Downs and the Sheep

A map of the Pitton district in 1773 shows a recognizable countryside. Indeed, even minor features are still readily identifiable. The Green, White Hill, High Street, Bove Hedges, Church Lane, Black Lane, Slate Way, Dunley Hill, Dirty Lane, Farley Lane and Cockroad are all clearly outlined as are Parsonage Farm, Manor Farm and Bowers Farm. Even the houses along Cold Harbour and at the bottom of Slate Way are marked.

But these are features in the village and on its southern side. To the north, north-east and north-west the map presents a very different picture. Bottom Way is outlined with a dotted line, indicating that it was not hedged and was regarded as a track rather than a road. The same applies to White Way, except the section actually in the village, and to Winterslow Hollow. And then, beyond Bottom Way and White Way are tracks which bear no relation to any existing today. There is quite a network of them, apparently linking the village with the Winterbourne valley, on the far side of the main Salisbury-London road, or with the prehistoric earthwork of Figsbury Ring.

The explanation is that all this area to the north of the village was open downland, the last section of Salisbury Plain. Here tracks were temporary. Horsemen, vehicles and sheep went where they would. When traversing the lonely downs, the traveller aimed to take the shortest possible cut, steering by sun and stars. A feature of the map to the north is the occasional pinpointing of a 'Direction Post', as welcome guide to a bemused pilgrim.

A bequest left by a once-benighted traveller on the downs to the church at Berwick St John (on the south-western edge of the Plain) to cause the church bells to be rung at sunset is a reminder of how difficult it was to navigate these bewildering downs. South of Salisbury the carrier to Whitsbury used to have his route over the downs marked by 'chalk lights' – pyramids of chalk erected at intervals. As on winter nights his cart drew level with one heap, the next was dimly discernible by the yellow light of his oil lamps.

Starting his working life as a shepherd boy at the age of fourteen, Ted Whitlock was entrusted with shepherding a flock of sheep across Salisbury Plain from Tilshead to Pitton, a journey of some fifteen miles. *En route* he had to cross two rivers, each with its narrow zone of meadows, hedges and arable, but, those apart, his route was entirely over the open plain.

'There I saw nothing but the downs and the sky,' he used to say. 'No fields, no hedges, no houses, no roads, no cultivation, no people, except for an occasional shepherd in the distance. No life at all, except for larks, the wheatears and the rabbits. I shaped my course by the sun and was glad when at last I could see from a distant hill the chalk cliffs of Pitton.'

The sheep kept were from hurdle flocks, for which special crops, chiefly turnips, were grown on the arable fields. Most of them in Wiltshire were of the Hampshire Down breed, though a couple of generations earlier they were Wiltshire Horns. Other breeds were almost unknown. Ted Whitlock remembered the commotion a batch of Scottish Blackface sheep caused when they first appeared at Wilton Fair in the 1890s.

In the heyday of the system the downland farms were run for the benefit of the sheep. For years ahead the farmer planned a succession of crops for their food, mainly turnips, vetches and clover. With hurdle folds moved daily, the shepherd rationed out what was available, letting the sheep into a fresh pen each morning.

Lambing was planned for February, an arrangement which allowed the young lambs to grow rapidly on the fresh spring grass and also to catch the summer market, when fat lamb prices were high. It did mean, however, a lambing season in the worst month of winter. Farmers who had sufficient room in their barns and other buildings constructed lambing pens there, but most of them had to make temporary pens in the arable fields. They chose a site as sheltered as possible, in a corner where two high hedges met and with often a straw rick to form a third side of a quadrangle. Along the inner sides of a spacious fold of wattle hurdles the shepherd constructed a series of individual pens or coops, each large enough for one ewe and her offspring. Often hurdles covered with straw served as a roof. As the lambs were born, the shepherd transferred each lamb with its mother to one of the coops, where both remained for several days. The couples were then moved to a separate part of the main fold reserved for them.

The shepherd's life during the six weeks or so of the lambing season tended to be exacting. He did the rounds every few hours during the night; nor did he normally delegate any of his duties by day. His headquarters for the period was his 'shepherd's hut' – a timber room on iron wheels, drawn up alongside the lambing pens. In it could be found his bed, a stove always burning, a plain table and a chair, a shelf for medicine bottles and ointment, and a few pegs for hanging clothes.

During the day the rest of the farm waited on him like workers tending a queen bee. He received daily visits from the water barrel, the hay waggon, general farmworkers engaged in repairs or pitching new hurdle pens, and, of course, the farmer himself, checking to see that all was well and bringing up provisions.

As soon as a sufficient bite of young grass had grown in the water-meadows, the sheep and lambs moved thither, the lambs being allowed first choice by means of a 'lamb creep' in the hurdle barrier – of the right size to permit a lamb to pass through but not a sheep. By May ample grass was available in all pastures. As some of these were laid up for mowing in June or early July, the sheep moved to arable crops grown especially for them, such as vetches and dredge corn (a mixture of oats and vetches or peas). June was also the shearing month.

After haymaking the lambs, now growing fat, remained in the arable fields, feasting on more crops grown for their benefit. The aftermath of seeds hay – a mixture of rye grass and red clover from which a hay-cut had been taken – and which was always a good stand-by. The ewes meantime moved to the open downs, which now assumed their traditional place in the farm economy.

An arable field, usually a hay aftermath, was generally reserved for their night quarters, but by day they roamed at will over the limitless downs. Here the shepherd watched his flock as in a pastoral idyll. Here he enjoyed the summer holiday which was his reward for the dark and bitter weeks in his spartan hut at lambing time. Not that he would have admitted for one moment that he was enjoying a holiday. No, he was a good shepherd, attending to his sheep.

All through harvest he would sit on a thyme-scented bank, meditating and watching his fellows in the fields down the hill labouring hard and long to get the harvest gathered. Sometimes, in a rare fine interval in a wet summer, they would cast envious glances in his direction and hint to the farmer, 'Can't old Shep come and gie us a hand?'

When hard pressed, the farmer might reluctantly and with careful forethought put the situation to the shepherd. A direct approach would be certainly met by a straight refusal: 'Be I shepherd or bain't I? I got to see to thee sheep, ha'n't I?' But with flattery and persuasion the desired end could sometimes be achieved. The shepherd had the whip hand, though. He knew that no farmer could afford to lose a competent shepherd.

Summer on the downs gave the shepherd ample leisure, which he used according to his interests. A popular pastime with shepherds was the carving of 'shepherds' sticks'. These were, in effect, short clubs or cudgels, such as those with which in even earlier times duels were fought. Back in the eighteenth century the shepherds from all over Salisbury Plain and the Dorset and Hampshire downlands attending Wilton Fair in October used to fight with these weapons for the title 'King of the Shepherds'. The crown went not to the most proficient shepherd but to the best fighter. On the night before the fair, after the combats had been resolved, the shepherds lay in a great circle on the floor of the fairground barn, their heads towards the centre of the circle and pillowed on their most valuable possession, their dog.

The shepherds' sticks were the only weapon permitted to the shepherd in the days when farmworkers were forbidden to arm themselves with anything that could be used to kill a pheasant. Ostensibly they were for the protection of the sheep against marauders of any sort. Actually they were very effective throwing-sticks. Beautifully balanced, with one end heavier than the other, in the hand of an expert they could be lethal. If, as he strolled alongside a hedge, the shepherd spotted a rabbit or a pheasant crouching in the undergrowth, he was sure of something for the pot the next day.

The shepherd's stick had another role, both utilitarian and artistic. Relaxing in the downs on a summer afternoon, he patiently carved on it, in low relief, pictures of whatever took his fancy. It might be portraits of his sheep, or a passing fox, or a soaring skylark, or his pen-knife, or the utensils in his hut. Or it might be more ambitious, as in one example which depicted a fox hunt, with the fox, the horses, the hounds, the huntsmen, a horn and riding whip, and the fox's brush. These shepherds' sticks were sold for pin-money at the autumn fairs, and a few still survive as collectors' pieces.

The shepherd also reckoned on shaping the yokes and accessories for his sheep-bells. The bells themselves were usually made by specialists – one of whom, whose surname was Lancaster, is still remembered in his home village of Cheverell, Wiltshire. Makeshift bells were, however, made from old tin cans, with an iron bolt and nut as a clapper. The yokes were turned from a boomerang-shaped piece of wood, ideally gorse with a natural angle, from which the bell was suspended by a strip of leather from old harness. It was fastened there by a wing-shaped peg, also fashioned by the shepherd with his pen-knife. Sometimes he chose to work on a piece of sheep bone. Sometimes he would take a wand of some very hard and durable wood, such as yew, and carve it into a series of connected pegs, so that he could snap one off as he needed. The patience and skill required for such a feat were phenomenal, but then, the shepherd had plenty of time.

Sheep-bells were needed only during the summer break on the downs; at all other times the sheep were kept under control by hurdle fences. While roaming over the downs they were allowed entirely free range and often wandered a mile or more from the shepherd. Even when they were out of sight, however, the shepherd kept in touch with them through the music of the bells.

For a flock of 200 or 300 sheep he would have ten or a dozen bells. These would be fastened on the recognized leaders of the flock, individuals whom the shepherd knew well. They were generally mature ewes who had been about for a few years and knew all the tricks. The other sheep would follow them. When the sheep were quietly grazing on the short, herb-rich turf, they would nibble for a moment or two, then move on a pace, and the bells would gently tinkle. The listening shepherd would know that all was well. At other times he would hear a rhythmic swinging – the sheep were on the march. Probably they were on the way to a pond for a drink, but, knowing the propensity of the leading ewes to take the flock into trouble, he would find it prudent to investigate. Occasionally there would come a horrid jangling. The sheep were being chased. With a sigh, the shepherd would lay down his pen-knife, call his dog and take up his cudgel. The likeliest culprit was an inoffensive fox, for stray dogs were rare in those days.

The end of the summer holiday on the downs came in September or early October. The ewes would then move down to the arable land, to be steamed up on turnips, meal and other nourishing food preparatory to meeting the ram in November, while the fat lambs went to market or fair.

Such was the traditional system of sheep-farming in downland England – the foundation of Victorian high farming. The sheep themselves produced two harvests a year – one of meat, the other of wool – besides manuring the arable fields with their droppings and so earning a worthwhile wheat crop the following year. Hence the term 'golden hoof'.

When from 1875 onwards this previously sound system staggered and finally collapsed, the farmers on the big downland sheep farms could not believe it. Pitton farmers in the period under survey were like the survivors of a tidal-wave disaster. Their world was still awash. All around them were reminders of the old, destroyed way of life in which they had been reared. They could not understand why it had foundered or what they were now supposed to do.

On most of the farms the sheep still lingered for the first two decades of the century, though not on the same scale as hitherto. By the end of the 1920s all had gone, except for the occasional agisted flocks pushed on Ted Whitlock's holding by the auctioneer. Old shepherds in the evening of their days lamented the passing of the once-familar scene.

One was Mark Collins, a pleasant and much-respected old man who in his heyday had been the leader of the

Pitton shearing gang. This was a group of about eight shearers who in early summer toured the farms of a wide district, shearing on contract. In the photograph, taken in 1883, Mark Collins is the character on the left. Others who are identifiable by persons now living and who therefore must have survived until the 1920s are Noah White and Albert White. When on tour a gang slept in farms and worked over an open fire outdoors – a pleasant enough break from the general farm routine.

A little later, around the turn of the century, Arthur Whitlock, with his son Charlie and his nephew Ted, joined the shearing gang, but before long they were recruited by John T. Woolley, the auctioneer, to do specialist shearing. That involved preparing pedigree sheep for shows, fairs and sales. Instead of shearing the entire fleece, with hand shears, of course, the expert concentrated on trimming around the head and tail and producing a flat, table-like back. The radius of their travels was now thirty or forty miles, and soon the trio were organizing the details of the fairs and sales. When Arthur retired, Charlie took a post as head shepherd to a pedigree flock, far from Pitton, but Ted continued to manage local sheep fairs and undertake trimming contracts for years after he had acquired his farm – in fact, until the late 1920s. His son Ralph (the author) remembers attending Britford Fair, near Salisbury, in about 1925. Ted spent the day before the fair supervising the lay-out of the hurdle-pens and allocating them to the various owners selling their sheep. On the morning of the fair he was on his way, shepherding a flock through the sleeping, dusky streets of Salisbury at 2.30 a.m.

As the old traditions of sheep-farming died away, few of the Pitton farmers invested in a proper sheepdog. It can be said, however, that there was no tradition of collies in this part of England. Arthur Whitlock remembered the stir created by the first specimens to appear at a local sheep fair.

Old bob-tailed English sheepdogs were the Wessex breed, but more numerous were the bearded collies, though not necessarily pure-bred. Arthur had a cross-bred dog of this type, Old Floss, whom he could leave in charge of his flock for hours at a time. All he had to do was take her around the boundaries over which the sheep were not to pass and he could go down to the village in perfect confidence.

4   The Woods and Woodland Workers

The woods to the south, east and west of the village were almost exclusively of hardwoods, mostly oak, though to a lesser extent of beech, with hazel underwood. As a general rule the oaks were thinly spaced, at no more than twenty to the acre, and the hazel was considered the more important crop, providing the owner with a cash income every seven or eight years. The Pitton woodmen were nearly all independent, self-employed men, who in autumn contracted with the estate-owner to buy the standing, mature hazel by the acre. An acre or so would supply sufficient underwood to keep the purchaser busy all the winter.

His first task when he started work in autumn was to build himself a little shelter, of hurdles and thatch. The hut was open on the south side, facing the sun, and around it the woodman stacked his wood as he cut it, soon completing a more or less weather-proof yard. Its furniture consisted of a chopping-block, a series of pole gauges and, for hurdle-makers, a frame. Usually a permanent fire for burning odd chips of wood was kept smouldering.

On fine days the woodman cut hazel on his plot, severing the rods by skilled down-cuts with his billhook. In wet weather he sat in his hut fashioning the rods into whatever his speciality might be. Hurdle-makers were the supreme specialists, always assured of a ready market for their wattle hurdles on local farms. Other woodmen made sheep-cribs, ladders and tool handles, though mostly they sold the cut rods to craftsmen with properly equipped workshops, of which several flourished in the neighbouring villages. All bound hazel of the appropriate size into bundles of pea-sticks and bean-rods and into firewood faggots. At one time a thriving trade was done in elongated bavins of brushwood, for use as ships' fenders in Southampton docks.

At Winterslow Mr Charlie Dear provided a market for much of the local underwood. He not only dealt in the usual commodities, such as hurdles, faggots and cottage requisites, but also had workshops for fashioning tool handles, rakes, sheep cribs, ladders and other farming accessories. One of the workshops was an old two-roomed cottage in which Charlie's elderly uncle, Isaac, worked on cold or wet days. He kept a fire burning on the hearth, on either side of which stood a well-worn armchair, one for his own use and the other almost permanently occupied by a black-and-white cat.

Charlie and Isaac were experts in the uses of the various home-grown woods. In addition to hazel the woodmen were permitted to cut ground ash, which are ash saplings thrusting up straight from the ground. Ash was in demand for the sides or poles of ladders and for frames and shafts of waggons. One of the first tasks an apprentice carpenter was given was to make a wheelbarrow of ash wood. Ash was ideal for all sorts of handles, including, in the old violent days of hand weaponry, the shafts of spears and pikes. One of its assets is that it does not splinter but wears smooth with handling. There used to be a steady demand for the hames fitted over the collars of horses' harness, and these were almost invariably made of ash, though latterly it was superseded by iron.

Ash, like hazel, can be cleft easily, and the cleft rods can be readily bent into shape. So in making sheep cribs, which are, in effect, light and portable mangers for hay, cleft ash rods were used for the long, straight bars, and cleft ash bent into a semi-circle for the ends. In earlier times thin strips of ash were bent into shape for the sides and bottoms of bushels, peck-measures and buckets.

An extremely skilled craft depending on ash rods was the making of sneads or snathes, which are the curved handles of scythes. After cleft ash had been roughly shaped by axe, it was steamed to render it pliable and then fastened by pegs and iron clamps to a 'setting pin'. For the finishing touches to a snead Charlie and Isaac Dear employed a home-made smoothing-plane which they called an 'engine', which produced a smooth, tapering handle.

Less exciting in their manufacture but still representing skilled workmanship were the hay-rakes, of which there were two main types – the light hay-rake and the heavier drag-rake requiring the use of both hands. Drag-rakes were used for gathering up into 'pooks' mown hay in the fields whereas the lighter rakes were, in effect, tidying-up tools, such as were used in raking down the sides of hay-ricks. These tools were entirely of ash, teeth being of cleft ash pegs.

In waggon-building the felloes (sections of the rims) were often of ash, and the same wood was frequently used for the sides and ladders. Housewives demanded that their clothes posts, for supporting a clothes line, should be of ash, and gypsies sometimes stole from the woodman's store cleft ash for making clothes pegs.

Apart from manufacturing hurdles and tying bundles of bean-rods, pea-sticks and faggots, the hazel of the underwood had one other primary use, the making of spar-gads. These are the spars, about two feet long, for fastening thatch to a roof, and in the days when virtually all roofs were of thatch, of ricks as well as of buildings, the demand for spars was unlimited. Even today the surviving spar-makers find plenty of work.

The faggots of brushwood, chiefly but not exclusively hazel, were used primarily as kindling wood and for heating cottage ovens. A whole faggot would be placed in the oven, lighted and allowed to burn to ashes. When the ashes were raked out, a fire-brick at the inner end indicated by glowing to a tint (which the experienced housewife could quickly recognize) that the oven was hot enough, the loaves were placed inside and the oven door was shut. Faggots were also in demand for the foundation of ricks, particularly of hay-ricks which were required to stand all the winter. They acted as insulating material, to prevent damp creeping up into the hay, and of course they could be burnt for firewood later.

Hazel, being so supple, can be twisted into bonds for tying bundles and was often used in this way, certainly for bundles of underwood. Woodmen kept an eye open for rods with a fork in an appropriate place to be cut for a thumb-stick, and boys appreciated similar forks for catapult handles. So did dowsers, for water-divining, though the forked sticks they employed were not necessarily of hazel.

A law of Edward IV, dated 1483 and probably sealing with Parliamentary approval a practice already established, permitted fences to be erected around coppiced woodland, meaning woodland in which hazel and other underwood was regularly cut. The purpose was to keep out not only deer but cattle and horses which would browse off the young shoots of the tree stubs and so prevent natural regeneration. The law allowed such a fence to remain for seven years, which, in view of what has already been written about coppicing practice, meant in perpetuity, for at the end of seven years the young rods were big enough to be cut and so the process started all over again. The peasants probably recognized it for what it was, a device to keep their livestock out of the woods and so cheat them out of some of their common land.

A parallel activity to coppicing was pollarding. Coppicing involved cutting off the sapling rods just above ground level, thus creating a 'stub' or 'stool' from which new shoots would grow. Pollarding meant sawing off the crown of a tree at a height from six to ten feet – usually in woodlands a good ten feet. The trunk would in due course send out new shoots from the point where it had been severed, but they would be out of reach of cattle and even of deer standing on their hindlegs, so pollarded trees required no fences. Pollarding was not confined to hazel and ash but was practised on almost all types of deciduous tree, notably oak, beech, elm, maple, lime and sycamore. Close examination of many old woodland trees will reveal evidence that they have at one time been pollarded. In Pitton pollarding was particularly practised on the paddock trees behind the farmsteads, the farmers placing an important value on the regular crop of saplings thus obtained.

Coppicing and pollarding in general provided a useful and regular income for whoever owned the trees so treated. Just before the period under review it was estimated that an estate-owner could expect a return of £15 an acre from his underwood once every seven or eight years. With agriculture in depression, he would be lucky to get anywhere near £2 an acre per year as rent for farmland. Incidentally, the woods in those days were kept neat and tidy, for the contract signed by the underwood workers included a clause that all brambles and weeds were to be cleared and burned before the site was vacated.

The proximity of these extensive woodlands had an impact on the general economy of the surrounding villages. Our illustration (see pp.64-5) shows a page from the account book of Noah White, who also appears in the photograph of the Pitton shearing gang in the 1880s. He is the figure in the right foreground.

Noah never possessed a horse and cart or even a

hand-barrow, so, like many of the woodmen, he relied on his neighbours (to most of whom he was related) to haul his faggots, hurdles and other commodities for him. Most of the farmers regarded wood haulage as a useful secondary income.

Though underwood work was the aspect of woodland activity which most directly concerned the villagers of Pitton, the larger timber also had its importance for the village. The village builders, who were also wheelwrights, were competent makers of carts and waggons, for which they required the planks of ash, beech and elm. The timber merchants, working in the woods on contract, not only sold them timber but also purchased timber carriages from them. They also hired horses from the farmers for timber hauling, – a strenuous job to which only the heaviest horses were equal.

Memories lingered of former woodland harvests. Though nutting (the gathering of hazel-nuts) was a popular autumn pastime with women and children, it was remembered that in earlier hard times the nuts had been collected for sale to bakers, who used them to augment supplies of flour in bread-making. The author recalls collecting bucketfuls of acorns under oaks on his father's farm for feeding to pigs, but the real reason for the exercise was to clear the acorns away before the cows could get at them. Cows are fond of acorns but can easily fall victim to acorn poisoning.

Another memory is of collecting sloes, not for flavouring sloe gin but for sale to chemists for some unrevealed purpose. This again was a task mainly for women and children. They cut down the bushes with billhooks and picked off the sloes into buckets. Landowners evidently had no objection to the destruction of the otherwise almost useless blackthorn, which, anyway, would soon shoot again.

A woodland craft in which Pitton doubtfully partici-pated but which played a prominent part in the economy of neighbouring Winterslow was truffle-hunting. Now selling for fantastic sums in London emporia, truffles (underground fungi) grow under certain trees, usually beech or oak. At Winterslow truffling had the status of a thriving local industry, providing, at certain seasons of the year, a livelihood for perhaps ten or a dozen families.

In 1860 it was important enough for the truffle-hunters to send a petition to Parliament asking that their dogs be exempted from a new annual tax of twelve shillings a year. 'We, being poor labouring men, living in a woody district of the county where there is a great many English truffles grow, which we cannot find without dogs, we do therefore keep and use a small poodle sort of dog wholy and solely for that and no other ... It has been carried on by our ancestors for generations without paying tax for the dogs.' Whether the exemption was granted is not known, but truffle-hunting was still carried on at the turn of the century and, to a small extent, until the Second World War.

The truffle-hunters ranged far and wide throughout the district, obtaining permission from landowners to operate wherever there were woods. One of the best known of them was Eli Collins, a picturesque and notable character for whom the Earl of Radnor, of Longford Castle, near Salisbury, had a velveteen uniform designed and tailored. Eli Collins and his truffle-hounds were one of the attractions with which the Earl liked to entertain his house-guests. They were well known, too, in the woods around Pitton.

The lack of interest in game exhibited by the truffle dogs commended them to estate-owners who were preoc-cupied with game preservation. Bags of game were their chief interest in maintaining their estates, far exceeding income from farm rents, and for a tenant farmer to be caught shooting or snaring a hare inevitably resulted in his being given notice to quit next Michaelmas. In spite of the penalties, which in earlier times included transport-ation, poaching was rife. Most villagers were born poachers. In the first half of the nineteenth century many of them took game out of necessity, to eke out a meagre standard of living. That consideration was still valid in the first decades of the twentieth century, but by then the chief motivation was sport. Outwitting vigilant keepers was a challenge which could not be ignored. And the woods around Pitton teemed with game.

The underwood workers had to be very careful. The keepers naturally kept an eye on them, and one mistake could banish them from the woods which were their livelihood. But many of them set snares in the hedgerows on their way to and from work. Cottagers whose living did not depend upon the estate-owners were bolder, though still circumspect. There were not many cottagers in Pitton who did not know the woods intimately enough to be able to negotiate them on a dark night.

1907	Noah White Recived	£	s
July 18	of Mr F Burtt on Houing	1	0
August 3	Noah White Recived of Mr F Burtt	1	0
14	Recived	1	0
15	Mr F Burtt 500 Yard Spars		
24	Noah Recived on Hizing Sheves	0	10
24 25 26	Noah White 3 Days & 3 qurters Hizing Sheves	13	9
September 6	Noah White Recived	1	0
Sep 30	Noah White Paid mrs John White For Spars	1	3
1907	Noah White		
Nov 1 & 2	2 Days Cutting in Mr F Burtt at 2s 4d Per Day	4	8
7 & 8	2 Days Cutting in The Isle Paid	4	8
January 17 1908	Noah White 150 lugs From A Bather		
January 23	Noah White Paid Alfred Battem For 150 lugs	5	15
Febuary 3	Noah White Recived of lews White on Cutting in Harley Coppice lot 4	1	10
Febuary 12	Noah White 1 load lugs From Mr F Parsons		
November 9 1909	Pig Club money	£23	16 1
January 4 1910			10 1
September Recived	Recived	£24	7 0

Our illustration is of a couple of pages from the leather-bound account book of Noah White, a typical underwood worker, in 1888.

		£	s	D
1907	John & Noah Whites at Begges Coppice			
	Mr J Kerely			
	20 Fagots			
	10 Bundles			
Feb	Mr J Burtt			
26	10 Dozen Hurdles Paid Feb 26	3	17	6
arch	Noah White			
14	~~Fagots~~ 15 Fagots			
	4 Hurdles & 1 Six Faint 2 B Short Pea Sticing			
pril 10	50 Bundles		4	6
	John White			
10	50 Bundles		4	6
	6 Bundles Pea Sticing		1	6
	Mr J Kerely			
10	50 Fagots		6	6
	George Callway Noah White Paid lews White For Cardge G Callway Bundles Oct 99			
11	50 Bundles and H Elkins Bean Sies		8	6
11	Henery Elkins 1 Bun Bean Stics and Bundle			
	Noah White May 22 Carddge Paid lugs Fagots			
April	20 & 22 3 loads lugs from Begges & Part of			
	Mr lews White from Begges			
April	13 Bundles Pea Sticing		2	8½
	6 Bundles Bean Sticing		2	6
may	Noah White Carddge Paid			

5   The Builders and Craftsmen

That a tradition of building and craftsmanship should develop in Pitton seems natural. True, there was no good building stone, but there was timber in abundance. The underwood crafts dealt with in the previous chapter were matched by the work of those who wrought in mature timber.

Thirty generations have marvelled at and been inspired by the exquisite perfection of Salisbury Cathedral and especially its tapering spire, wondering at the temerity of those architects and masons who dared to pile up massive stonework to a height of 404 feet. But they were equalled in skill by the builders and carpenters who constructed the timber framework of scaffolding. Indeed, so integral a part of the edifice did this become that in the end some of it was retained, for its strength, and still holds together the masonry.

Most of the stone was fetched by horse and waggon from the quarries at Chilmark, in the Nadder Valley, but plenty of timber was available nearer the site. Much of it undoubtedly came from the forests of Clarendon and Penchet, and it seems likely that Pitton villagers were among the woodland workers who felled, hauled and perhaps shaped it.

Just beyond the horizon of our period there were two builders in Pitton, the Brieants and the Pitts. The Pitts lived in the thatched house now known as Peartree Cottage; the Brieants in Church House, which one of the family built just behind the church. Both flourished in the last decades of the nineteenth century, but business evidently went sour on Lewis Brieant, who disappeared from the scene in the 1890s.

'Disappeared from the scene' is an accurate phrase, for one day he vanished from his familiar haunts and was never seen in Pitton again. No one, not even his family and certainly not his creditors, knew where he had gone, though years later there came news, or perhaps rumours, that he had shaped a new life for himself in America. When he walked out of Pitton, it was said, he went to board a ship at Southampton.

Local tradition supplies a few details about the downfall of the Brieants. The lime-kilns were, it is said, constructed on 'life-land', meaning land held for a period of years determined by the lives of three named persons. When the last life mentioned in the lease ended, the site reverted to the landowner, presumably the Earl of Ilchester, who thereupon offered to allow the Brieants, whose head was named Charles, to continue using the kilns at a rent of £10 a year. Charles refused and quit. Afterwards the Earl's agent offered the kilns to him at a nominal rent but, like so many of the Pitton villagers, Charles was a stubborn man. And so the lime-kilns fell derelict.

The Pitts, however, continued in business until just before the First World War. Older residents remember when a wheelwright's table was the central feature of the yard, now a lawn in front of Peartree Cottage, with a range of workshops on either side.

The Brieants were apparently responsible for another important feature of Pitton, though perhaps the process was begun by even earlier builders. After a 'Profile' of the village appeared in the *Salisbury Journal* in 1987, a correspondent from Porton sent to the editor a humorous letter objecting that there had been a notable omission – the article had omitted to mention Pitton Docks! From the downs above Porton, and from many other eminences, he said, the white cliffs of the harbour were a conspicuous feature of the landscape. There is a pun here on 'Cold Harbour' which runs along the base of the hill, and the white cliffs of Pitton seem associated in the writer's mind with the White Cliffs of Dover. But the cliffs themselves, dazzling white until within the last few decades (when they have become overgrown by vegetation), rise like ramparts on either side of the aptly named White Hill.

Between the wars chalk was still dug there by the village farmers, especially on the east side of the hill. A small sum per load was paid to Reg Eyres, who farmed the land on the cliff top and whose property was apt to shrink by under-mining. Some of the farmers, however, were content with the rubbly chalk which had been dislodged by earlier quarrying and which formed a scree at the base of the cliffs. As the chief use they made of it was chalking thin soils, as a substitute for lime, it was probably just as effective.

The other side of the hill road was occupied by a series of lime-kilns which, at least in the last stage of their history, were worked by the Brieants. They had fallen into disuse some years before Lewis Brieant decamped, but in the 1930s villagers told their children how they themselves, as children, used to play hide-and-seek in the old kilns. It was possible, too, to detect the existence of a much earlier kiln flue on the eastern cliff.

To the lime-kilns Pitton owes much of its present topography. As has been noted, the village probably grew up around the pond and the church. The best farmsteads – Manor Farm, Parsonage Farm, Lodge Farm and Bowers Farm – all lay on that side of the village which faced the south and so enjoyed maximum sunshine. Church Farm, Taylor's Farm, Cold Harbour Farm and Webbs Farm established themselves on the floor of the valley. Only Ivyclad Farm and White Hill Farm, which were of comparatively recent origin and which, anyway, had not begun their life as farms, nestled under the hill. Most of the cottages, too, grouped themselves quite spaciously around their parent farms. But the really congested quarter of the village lay at the foot of White Hill, just below the lime-kilns. Here, with hardly room for a garden each, clustered no fewer than eighteen cottages, most of them perched on banks. What had happened was that these cottages had been built, some of them perhaps by squatters, on odd corners of land which no one bothered to claim. Life in them, under clouds of chalk dust and lime, must have been distinctly unattractive when the lime-kilns were going full blast.

Although it has been mentioned that Pitton, like most downland villages, had no building stone, it did possess, in addition to timber, a natural building material. This was chalk cob, of which many examples are still to be seen in cottages and garden or farmyard walls in the village. Building in chalk cob was, however, so much a Do-It-Yourself operation that it tended to be beneath the interest of the professional builders. Cottagers were expected to build their own cottages.

May was the month for cottage-building. It offered the advantage of long, light evenings at a time when the farms were not too busy. April was bedevilled by days of frosts, June brought haymaking, which in a wet summer had a tendency to linger on into harvest. In May a man could leave the hoeing at five o'clock and, after a bite for tea, have several hours to spare before nightfall.

The site having been secured, by negotiation, purchase or simply squatting, the young man with thoughts of matrimony assembled his able-bodied relations and friends and set to work. The first step, apart from marking out the site and digging the foundation, was to accumulate a good supply – several cart-loads – of rubbly chalk. No need to bother about drains, water pipes or electricity cables – such refinements were far in the future. As a matter of fact, even the foundations had an option about them. Theoretically, the cottage ought to be built on a course of flints, some two or even three feet deep and extending to several inches above ground level, but builders in a hurry (as they often were) dispensed with the flints and simply filled the trenches with chalk rubble. No damp-courses – a deficiency which condemned many of them to demolition when, in the 1950s, planning regulations were enforced.

Adjacent and as near as possible to the site, the builders made a heap of the chalk. Fixing iron soles, or pattens, to the boots, they began to tread it to achieve the right consistency. Buckets of water were poured on the mess as they trod, and horse-hair and/or wheat chaff were mixed in if available. The recognized procedure was for the men to circle clockwise, keeping to a steady rhythm, and Ted Whitlock recalled that there was a Mudwalling Song which they used to chant, though he could not remember the words or the tune. 'But then I was only a boy when I heard it.' It could have been a song of great antiquity, for, oddly enough, a tourist in Brittany, where the old craft evidently still survives, reports seeing peasants working in this way and chanting a song as they marched around.

When the paste had reached the required consistency, the workers dug into it and slapped it into position on the foundations. The tool used was a mud-walling prong – a heavy, flat-grained prong like Neptune's trident. They took no pains to make a neat job, being content to pile it up quickly before it set. A course about eighteen inches high could be added in an evening; any attempt to make it higher would cause the paste to start collapsing under its own weight. The wall had then to be left for a couple of evenings, to dry. Examination of surviving walls which have lost their plaster facing reveal the courses, like layers of stone or brickwork, of which they are constructed.

Building a mud wall was a laborious task, and time was short. The essentials were four walls, a chimney and a thatched roof, with bedrooms and stairs unless a bungalow-type hut was planned. When the walls on either side of the doorway were high enough for the prospective householder to stand against them without his head projecting over the top, it was time to put in the lintel – which is evidence that our ancestors tended to be shorter than we are, and why we often have to bow our heads when entering old cottages.

The logical way of building a cob wall would have been to heap the cob into a board mould, and this was the method adopted in the latest phases of the craft – just before and just after the First World War. But it was not commonly employed in earlier times, the probable reason being that the agricultural labourers who built the cottages had little board to spare. Instead the walls were trimmed level by great wooden saws. Somehow or other, they had to obtain timbers for doorposts, chimney corners, rafters, beams, joists, doors and windows. As the builders were mainly farmworkers, the farmer would usually provide most of these essentials, most likely through granting the men permission to cut the timber in his wide hedgerows to the south of the village.

Interior walls were generally of hurdlework with a coating of plaster. So, astonishingly, was the chimney. Chimneys investigated when so many of the old cottages were destroyed in the decades after the Second World War had their interior of hurdles *unplastered*. In some instances this wattlework was inches deep in soot, and that it survived for a century or two without going up in flames is miraculous.

Although the tradition of building cottages in cob or mud belonged, to some extent, to the labourers who would live in them, it was not entirely confined to them. In a district lacking building stone, the technique was used by professional builders as well. Most of the older houses in Pitton were an amalgam of cob and brickwork, the major exceptions being Manor Farm and Parsonage Farm. Most of the other farmhouses seemed to have been reshaped at various times, sometimes the additions being of brick and sometimes the original brick being supplemented by cob. Bowers Farmhouse and its satellite cottage were half-timbered in typical Tudor or Stuart styles, but the replacement of most of the exterior panels by brickwork gave them a more modern appearance. The interior walls, however, were entirely of hurdlework, concealed by plaster.

In Manor Farm and Parsonage Farm, together with most of their outbuildings, brick was dominant, and the roofs were tiled. At Clarendon Palace, some of the latest buildings were of bricks and, constructed in the reign of Henry VI, were said to be among the earliest examples of brickwork in England. It may have been at this time or soon afterwards that suitable clay measures between Farley and Clarendon began to be exploited. These brickworks were certainly flourishing in the nineteenth and early twentieth centuries, at a site appropriately known as Brickkiln Farm, and were major suppliers to local builders, who thus had an alternative to chalk cob at their disposal.

Building in chalk cob experienced a short-lived revival locally in the late nineteenth and early twentieth centuries. Bentley Farmhouse and several quite substantial houses and cottages in Pitton, and many more in Winterslow, were constructed of that material, notably those built by a Winterslow property-developer, Mr A. Clough. His houses were particularly distinguished by a mansard roof of tiles. At some time towards the end of the nineteenth century, Pitton builders began to use slates. Lewis Brieant's new house, Church House, for instance, had a slate roof, and several cottages, when the roofs needed repairs, had the thatch stripped off and replaced by slate.

During the 1914-18 War the Army authorities became interested in the properties of chalk cob. They rounded up surviving practitioners and transported them to barracks on Salisbury Plain to instruct soldiers in the technique. Apparently they had in mind the possibility of rapidly constructed defences for the trenches on the Western Front, but chalk cob was too fragile a material and tended to disintegrate too easily, so the scheme came to nothing. After the War the older generation of mudwallers passed away without transmitting their skills.

The Pitton building firms did not, of course, confine their activities to the village. They operated in villages for miles around. And occasionally builders from other villages undertook contracts in Pitton. The new wing of Ted Whitlock's house, later known as White Hill Farm, was erected by Josh Parsons, of Farley, though in this instance the fact that he was Ted's brother-in-law was undoubtedly the deciding factor.

In addition to building houses, chapels and village halls, however, the Pitton builders were noted waggon-builders. At many a Michaelmas farm sale buyers would look for the inscription 'Pitt & Son' on farm waggons or carts they were thinking of purchasing, and seeing it were reassured. Waggon-building was a highly skilled craft – or, rather, a combination of crafts, for a well-built waggon owed much to the blacksmith and carpenter as well as to the master builder. As already mentioned, the woods required for the various parts of the carriage were rigidly prescribed – elm for the nave of a wheel; well-seasoned oak for the spokes; beech for the axles; ash for the shaft, felloes and side planks; oak for the frame; elm for the bed; and so on.

Some of the craftsmen employed in this skilled work were self-employed. Censuses of the late nineteenth century refer to master builders, journeymen carpenters or bricklayers, sawyers and turners. They all worked for the building firms, but the master builders on contract rates, whereas the journeymen were employed at day rates. Sawyers and turners were self-employed but attached to the building firms. The turners of earlier decades had disappeared by the beginning of the period under review, but the village still had one sawyer, George Eyres. He lived in a house, still standing, at the corner of White Hill and The Green and worked in a sawpit in a shed opposite.

By 1915 Pitts had ceased to operate from Pitton, and the only building firm was Eyres & Son, whose headquarters was Ivyclad Farm, so George Eyres, brother of Reg, was stationed on the edge of the family establishment.

After the war Alec Pearce of Winterslow, a young man returning from army service, took over much of the Pitt business. Old Edward Eyres, the head of the firm, died, and his son Reg concentrated on farming, leaving Pearce's as the sole local builder. His workshop and yard extended along the southern side of Black Lane, though later, after the death of Toby Whitlock, he took over the house and buildings of Lodge Farm.

Included in the sheds by Black Lane was the village smithy, a sooty old forge with a galvanized iron roof. The blacksmith was a young man, Len Kerley, who after a time found the business side of his profession uncongenial and so handed it over to Alec Pearce, who was happy to employ him. Much of his work consisted of shoeing farm horses and repairing farm machinery; every horse in the village was a regular visitor to the smithy. However, though possessing the bulging muscles of the conventional blacksmith, Len was not otherwise strong and was frequently away ill.

Directories of the late nineteenth century recorded no fewer than three shoemakers and one 'cordwainer', which presumably was the same thing. By the early twentieth century none was left, and villagers had to send their shoes for repair to someone at Farley. After the 1914-18 War an ex-serviceman, Frank Linzey, settled for a time in Pitton, and early in the 1940s George Baker, evacuated from Hastings, became the village shoe-repairer. Repairs only were then undertaken, though the earlier shoe-makers really made shoes. 'They were as heavy as men's hobnails, and they never wore out!' complained the girls.

A trade or profession that came into existence in the later years of the nineteenth century was bakery. Earlier almost every housewife baked her own bread, in bread ovens which were an integral part of chimney corners, but at some time – probably in the 1890s – Jabez Laversuch set up a village bakery in the brick-and-tiled cottage still known as 'The Old Bakery'. When our period opens, the bakery was run by Uriah Whitlock and his family, which conprised himself, his brother Walter, his sister Mary-Ann and an invalid widowed sister, Sarah.

The bakehouse was a low brick building set at right angles to the rear of the house and flanking one side of a yard, the other side of which was occupied by stables. There Uriah kept a pony and trap with which he used to deliver bread and groceries to Farley and to the outlying farms and cottages on the Clarendon estate. Walter, known locally as 'Old Baker', pushed a black, lidded hand-barrow around the village with the Pitton deliveries.

As an adjunct to the bakery, the women turned their front room into a shop. There Mary-Ann, known to the whole village as 'Aunt Polly', presided behind a board counter. Her stock in trade was basic, comprising such essentials as loaf-sugar, tea, bar soap, soda, cheese, matches, bootlaces and assorted hard-boiled sweets. Senior villagers remember going as children to the shop for a ha'peth of sweets and seeing Aunt Polly bite a pear-drop in half to get the exact weight! The other half was returned to the big glass jar for the next customer.

Uriah and Mary-Ann played a prominent part in village life. Uriah, a slim, wiry man with side-whiskers, was said 'to have a good head on him' and was known as 'lawyer'. He engaged in local politics as an enthusiastic Liberal. Both he and Mary-Ann were active chapel people. Walter, a bent and stooping old man, tended to be a passenger, and the invalid Sarah was seldom seen.

Morris Baugh, the thatcher, lived in one of the Cold Harbour cottages at the beginning of the period but shortly after the war moved to a semi-detached cob-and-thatch cottage by The Green. Morris and his wife Annie had two sons, Morris and Albert. He himself was the son of Stephen Baugh, a small farmer, and was the brother-in-law of William Clark. Self-employed, he was also self-taught. Nevertheless he was quite competent to tackle all the thatching work the village offered, and cottages, farmhouses, farm buildings and the annual crop of ricks were enough to keep him busy. On wet days in winter he sat in the lean-to shed at the side of his cottage, shaping thatching spars.

The only other craft of which there is any recollection is 'rhining'. A woodland craft, this consisted of stripping the bark from young oaks when the sap was rising in April, for use in tanning leather. There was a saying that, 'A piece of "rhine" as big as a penny was worth a penny.' The craft was once carried on in the local woods, but Reuben Collins, the last local practitioner, had to walk over to the New Forest to exercise it in the last phase.

6 Cottagers and Others

Under the Ilchester regime nearly every house in the village belonged to the estate. The exceptions were a small number of lifehold cottagers. A villager who had saved a bit of money and was burdened with an independent mind would negotiate with the agent for the lease of a plot of land on which he proposed to build a cottage. In return for an agreed sum, the agent would grant him the use of the property for the duration of, say, three lives. A standard example was the father of a young family who registered the property in the names of his three young sons. That happened with William Collins, who built Pond Cottages, on the opposite side of the road to Aymer's

Pond. When eventually the last of the three died, the property reverted to the landowner. Whoever was then occupying the cottage at that date usually continued to do so, though now having to pay rent to the estate.

Older residents remember hearing of the case of old 'Frosty' Parsons who found himself caught in such a predicament. When Emanuel Parsons, the agent, came to inform him of his changed status and to collect the first rent, Frosty let drive at him with a twelve-bore gun. Fortunately he missed.

In general, though, the villagers had long ago come to terms with the arrangement. It was part of the stable background to their lives.

Just as certain fields were traditionally attached to a certain farmstead, so certain cottages were traditionally allocated to agricultural labourers working on that farm. The farmer rented them from the estate, and the labourers occupied them either at a nominal rent or as part of their terms of employment. In many instances, a cottage, or a farm for that matter, would be occupied by the same family for several generations.

Not always, however. Though farm tenancies were dated from Michaelmas, it wasn't often that farms changed hands in Pitton, but a certain number of cottages did fairly regularly. There were farmers who stuck to their labourers for year after year, but others preferred a change. So Michaelmas was house-moving time. Furniture was manhandled out of a cottage and heaped on a farm waggon, with a rick-cloth to cover it if rain threatened. Then away over the hill went the family, out of the lives of the Pitton folk for ever. Or usually so. Sometimes, of course, romance involving these migratory families developed – probably a salutary occurrence, preventing the population from becoming too inbred.

In any case, the Michaelmas migrations were generally confined to a restricted group of villages. The newcomers who in due course came trundling down the hill in *their* waggons were strangers, but not strangers from distant parts.

When at the Sale the Pitton farmers bought their farms,

many of them bought also the cottages traditionally attached to those lands. Bowers Farm, for instance, had a satellite cottage almost adjoining the farmhouse; Cold Harbour Farm cottages were situated in the farm fields well away from the village. Other families, however, took the opportunity to acquire a house of their own, some settling for the one they were occupying and some moving to another which attracted them more. Many of those for which there was lukewarm demand were purchased at bargain prices by the retiring agent, Emanuel Parsons, as investments for his daughters. A pair of semi-detached cottages fetched around £50 each and were let to their occupants at the going rate of a shilling or a half-a-crown a week.

When the dust had settled, the village had assumed the appearance and character so well remembered by those who were children just after the First World War and who are now in their seventies.

Apart from Parsonage Farm and Manor Farm and the school, no houses or indeed buildings at all existed in the north-western sector of the village. The now populous Bove Hedges and Black Lane were empty. The three cob-walled, slate-roofed cottages still known as Island Cottages between Black Lane and Church Lane were there, though subsequently they have been vastly improved. Their occupants, reading from north to south, were Noah Whitlock and his family, Noah White and his wife Maria, and old Mr Legge and his middle-aged children, Alice and Sid Bush.

Noah Whitlock was then an old man but is thought to have been, at one time, a carrier and haulier – with horses, of course. Noah White, featured in the shearing gang picture, was an independent labourer, occupied in the woods in winter and doing seasonal work on the farms in summer. He, like his neighbour, Mr Legge, was now retired, except that he possessed a portable cider-press which he trundled around to the village orchards in autumn. Mr Legge's daughter, Alice Bush, kept house for the bachelor vicar, the Reverend C.M. Gay, at The Wardenry, Farley, and spent most of her time there. Sid

Bush, nicknamed 'Kymo', was a weak-backed, gangling man of no great intellectual capacity. For a time, when cow-keeping became a necessity, he was employed by Ted Whitlock as dairyman.

Alec Pearce moved into Church House in the early 1920s. Its previous occupants were the Talbot family, though the house was built by Brieants as a residence for the curate – a short-lived state of affairs. Tucked away between Church House, Lodge Farm and Island Cottages a fairly new brick-and-slate house, with a restricted garden, was the home of Arthur Mills and his wife. A neat and dapper man always well dressed and with his moustache carefully trimmed, Arthur was a master craftsman, either a carpenter or a bricklayer. He had married into the Eyres family and worked for them, though nearing retirement age. He and his wife had five handsome daughters and four sons, the eldest of whom, Reg, married the daughter of Walt Whitlock, of the Bakery.

On the other side of the church, Willow Cottage, a half-timbered, thatched cottage of attractive appearance, stood in nearly an acre of land, comprising orchard, paddock, garden and a shed or two and overlooking Aymer's Pond. It was evidently, and still is, one of the oldest cottages in the village, quite possibly of Tudor date. Here lived a celebrated Pitton character, Arthur Whitlock.

Arthur it was who graduated from being a shepherd to become the right-hand man of John T. Woolley, the auctioneer. His life was spent with sheep, but hearsay has it that pheasants, hares and other game took an easy second place. A typical story concerns his encounter at the Pheasant Inn with two Londoners. Said the landlord,

'I've got two smart chaps in the bar with a greyhound they want to set after a hare. Can you help?'

'Wait a bit,' said Arthur, 'and I'll see what I can do.'

In the inn stable he extracted a hare, which by some unexplained means had found its way into his bag, and skinned it. By devious means he coaxed the inn cat within range, grabbed it, fastened the hare's skin on it and stuffed it in his bag.

'Right,' he signalled to the innkeeper.

When the sportsmen emerged, he explained to them that in his bag he had a hare which he would release when they were ready. They had to have their hound ready on the leash, for the hare would be gone like a shot the moment the bag was opened. He took the precaution of collecting a guinea apiece from them in advance.

Immediately he tipped the cat out of the bag, it streaked across the yard, the greyhound on its tail. The cat naturally shot up the nearest tree, where it clung, spitting. The sportsmen looked around for an explanation from Arthur, but he had disappeared.

'I would have liked to stay,' he said, 'but I thought about my supper at home gettin' cold.'

And in telling the story afterwards he used to add, 'I often thought I would have liked to hear they two chaps tellin' their mates up in Lunnon of how down in Wiltshire there were hares wot climbed trees!'

He used to relate that his was a double wedding. The girls were sisters and cousins to the two bridegrooms, Arthur and Daniel, who were also cousins to each other. Arthur's family consisted of a son and four daughters, including a twin. Three of the daughters became Salvation Army officers.

A handsome, burly man who used the Wiltshire dialect with the authentic, high-pitched accent, he was highly intelligent. He excelled in telling high-faluting yarns with a perfectly straight face. It was widely believed that he was not a true son of his family, that there was a mystery about his paternity, involving one of the local gentry, but of course no one ever knew.

The cottage adjoining Bowers Farm was occupied at the time of the Sale by old Stephen Seaward and his wife, who had moved into it to allow their daughter and her husband, Jack Gower, to occupy the farmhouse.

On the opposite side of the road, at the far end of a paddock known as Sinnett's Close, Arthur White and his family lived in a new brick-and-tiled house. Arthur was a woodman, though now retired. He is remembered as a handsome old man with a magnificent white beard. Those

Pitton from the south in the 1920s

Pitton church in the early Twenties from the site on which Cherry Tree
Cottage was later built

The first Carnival Queen,
Hilda Pearce in 1936. She
later became Ralph's wife

Model Farm. Note the well-head

Ralph Whitlock with his tame badger Barney

Elsie Whitlock at the gate of Box Cottage

Bonny in bonnets: Millie and Susie Whitlock

With Christmas Greetings

Christmas greetings from Elsie Whitlock (*right*) and her fellow Salvation
Army officer, *c.*1939

Cows dragging their way up
White Hill on a frosty
morning

Tom Collins and his son Sam in the early 1920s

Ted Whitlock with Gipsy in 1918

Lavender Cottage, the original farmhouse of Taylor's Farm. Note the well-crib in the left foreground, and the sign 'LETTERBOX' over the window which indicates that the cottage was at one time the village post office

Emily Mills at Pond Cottage, *c.*1920

who witnessed him signing his name say he did it with a perfect copperplate hand but took a quarter of an hour to do so.

The semi-detached Pond Cottages, at right angles to the road and to Aymers Pond, were occupied during the war by young married couples, Alec and Annie Pearce and Lewis and Emily Mills. In the mud-walled though ivy-clad cottages with a slate roof were born the children of both families, who have helped considerably with information for this book. With the Mills lived old John Webb, Emily's uncle. A saintly old man, who was a leader at Pitton chapel for many years, he had reached retirement age well before the passing of the Act providing the first old-age pensions in 1910 and so needed to be still gainfully employed. So he had been appointed parish roadman, his chief duty being to fill in pot-holes and ruts with flint stones gathered from the fields. He also mowed the roadside verges with a scythe, drying the herbage for hay, which he pushed home in a kind of barrow and made into a little rick under the great spreading apple tree in the garden. In his eighties the poor old chap fell a victim to whooping cough, an ailment which he had escaped when young. It tried his frail body so severely that he never recovered.

Beyond Church Farm a footpath through a paddock known as Abbot's Close links the High Street with The Green. On the far side, the southern side, a cottage adjoined the Bakery, but this was pulled down and replaced at some time early in the present century, though whether before or after the Sale is not known. The new house typical of those erected by Mr Clough, was cob-walled with a tiled mansard roof. It was an elegant building, set in a spacious garden. The old, dismantled cottage had been the home of a family named Baugh, of one of whom, William Baugh, much will be told in a later chapter (p.129).

The cob-and-thatch house next door to the Bakery, now known as Pear Tree Cottage, was one of the 'big houses' of the village, as might be expected of the headquarters of the Pitt family. Memory seems uncertain about who occupied it at the time of the Sale, but in the 1920s a family named Swann lived there.

Up a long garden path behind the Pitt carpenters' shops were two thatched cottages, now amalgamated to create an attractive residence known as Apple Tree Cottage. They were then far from attractive, being untidy, dilapidated dwellings which would have seemed prize targets for demolition. Typical farmworkers' cottages, one was permanently occupied by an elderly bachelor, though it was generally assumed that the dame who lived with him was wife in all but name. Though his name was Jim Fry, he was known to everybody as 'Billy Lazarus' – 'Lazarus' for the reason that he once disappeared for a few years and was reputed dead, but then returned, full of life, but why 'Billy' instead of Jim no one could explain. The other cottage was reserved for migratory families, who worked for a year or so on one of the farms and then moved on.

Nearer the road and almost hiding the two cottages from view, a brick-and-thatch cottage was the home of George Collins and family. George, whose family of three boys and a girl had grown up, worked as carter for Owen Griffin. His cottage had no back garden, and so his winter woodpile, the adjunct of every Pitton cottage, had to be built at the front and side.

Box Cottage, the next range of buildings, was much nearer the road, which it overlooked from a vantage point of a bank surmounted by a large and neatly clipped box hedge – hence the name. Here lived another Collins family – Reuben, his wife Polly and children Bertram, Ethelind, Len, Frank, Evelyn and Alf. Reuben was a cousin of George and has already been mentioned as one of the last practitioners of the woodland craft of rhining. He was also master of other woodland crafts.

The term 'range of buildings' was used advisedly, for a second cottage adjoined Box Cottage. It was a somewhat cramped edifice, consisting of only one room (and a 'back place') downstairs and two upstairs. Its resident was Joby Compton, the last scion of an old Pitton family. A slightly built character in none too robust health, Joby boasted a bushy black beard and always wore a bowler hat, grey with age. He was afflicted by an atrocious stammer, which rendered him often the butt of ridicule, though mostly good-natured. When tormented, he quickly lost his temper and spluttered, 'I've had enough. I'll go to Tasmania.' Apparently other members of his family had emigrated to Tasmania.

Villagers used to relate how a stranger once asked the way of Joby, who, thus accosted and made nervous by the very presence of a stranger, contorted his features and had difficulty in getting out a single word.

'God bless the man! I could get there while you're telling!' exclaimed the man impatiently.

'Bloody well go on wi' ee!' said Joby, without the trace of a stammer!

Adjoining Joby's cottage stood another building, cob-walled with a tiled roof, which the Collinses used as a storehouse and bicycle shed. Although a bungalow type and consisting of only two rooms, it had once been the home of a family with several children. The last residents were a Mr and Mrs Offer – another old Pitton name – who lived there until their deaths.

Until not many years before the Sale the paupers of the village – outpatients of the workhouse – were entitled to a weekly allowance of five shillings and two loaves of bread. Their pittance was brought out from Salisbury once a week by a workhouse inmate and a relieving officer in a dusty old van drawn by a decrepit horse. Mary Offer's cottage was his port of call in Pitton. Ted Whitlock's mother, who had lost her husband in a tragic mishap when her boy was only six months old, was one of the recipients, and Ted could remember going down to meet the workhouse van at Mary's cottage. He remembered the loaves of bread, too, which, according to his account, were greyish, insipid stuff, guaranteed to kill any appetite.

Leap-frogging over Cold Harbour Farm, Lavender Cottage, rebuilt of brick and slate in 1924-5, stood in a spacious garden studded with apple trees. At one time it had been the village post office, but when surviving memory begins it was the home of a young man,

Willoughby Talbot, who had married a daughter of Arthur Mills and who through the 1920s raised his family there. Willoughby was a schoolmaster, teaching boys at one of the Salisbury schools. A short but strong and athletic man, he cycled to and from Salisbury – a six-mile journey each way – every day for many years. It was long remembered how, when a cottage by White Hill caught fire, Will broke all records by cycling to Salisbury in twenty minutes to fetch the fire brigade. It was a vain journey, for the cottage burned down before the fire engine arrived.

Will was also an enthusiastic bee-keeper and was one of those talented persons who seem able to handle bees with impunity. Working without gloves or veil, he would pluck bees from his face and even his eyelids without seeming to notice their stings. The son of Abram Talbot, who had come to Pitton as gamekeeper for the Earl of Ilchester, he always retained his love of gamekeeping and liked nothing better than patrolling a beat with his gun and dogs.

Rounding the corner, the road to White Hill passes first Webb's Farm, then, on the opposite side of the road, Model Farm, and then the chapel. Tucked away behind the chapel, a long path being the only access, are a pair of cob, brick and slate cottages of no great antiquity. Rose Cottages. When this story begins, the one nearer the road was occupied by Will Talbot's father, old Abram Talbot. He had come to the village years before as gamekeeper to Lord Ilchester and had his antecedents on one of the Earl's other estates. Now he was old and blind, Pitton's only blind man. The children of that time remember him as a figure who used to spend long hours by the gate, listening to familiar sounds.

The farther cottage was the home of Mark Collins, woodman and head of the shearing gang. Mark, too, was an old man, who died during or just after the war, but his wife outlived him by many years. Rose Cottages were thus a quiet little backwater for old people.

Before Edward Shellum bought the cob-and-thatch cottage now known as Lea Cottage, it was a farm cottage housing ephemeral families who made only a very temporary impact on the life of the village. It was a neglected and dilapidated house, with a beaten earth floor.

We now come to a cluster of cottages at the foot of White Hill, at the junction with The Green and the Cold Harbour footpath. As already noted, the site, so near to the dust-spewing lime-kilns, was so undesirable and insalubrious that squatters were able to operate unchecked. The cottages, nearly all cob-and-thatch though with patches of much-used brick, were crammed in close together, higgledy-piggledy, perched on banks with little scope for gardens.

A centrepiece was White Hill Farm, though at the beginning of the period it did not bear that name. It was simply another cob-and-tile cottage, later, in 1921, enlarged by Ted Whitlock, with a brick-and-slate extension. A diagonal path leading from the road corner led past two other cob-and-thatch cottages, used during the 1920s and 1930s by Ted Whitlock as farm stores, though they had been inhabited shortly before. One of them had at one time been the village post office.

On a triangular bank adjoining the hill and overlooking White Hill Farm were no fewer than five cottages. Two perished by fire at the very beginning of our period, it being alleged that one of the housewives emptied hot ashes in her woodshed. Two, perched on a terrace which gave a magnificent view across the valley to Clarendon Woods, were normally occupied by farmworkers. In the farther one lived Lewis Parsons and his sister Sophie Cox, both illiterate and mentally backward. Before our period begins, the other was the home of a one-legged veteran of the Crimean War – the father, in fact, of Uriah Whitlock who later kept the village shop. Then it was occupied by a widow, Mrs Downer; then by Percy Whitlock (son of Noah) and his family; then by Walter Parsons and his family, who came from some ten miles away to take a job on one of the farms. The fifth house, now White Hill Cottage, had more garden than most and was picturesquely situated. At the beginning of the story it was occupied by Ted Whitlock's mother, Jane, but when she

died it became the home of Mrs Ayres, whose husband
was killed in the war.

On the opposite side of the road, pressed against the
hillside and the grove of yews known as Monkey's Castle,
were two more cottages, thatched and mostly of cob. These
too were burned down, in the early 1920s. The cause of the
conflagration was no mystery: the thatch was set alight by a
spark from the chimney of a passing threshing-engine.
That was a familiar hazard much dreaded by the villagers.
When the threshing-machine was on its rounds, prudent
cottagers made sure they had a ladder handy and as many
buckets of water as possible. They watched the steam
engine anxiously until it was safely past, but in this instance
all their precautions were in vain.

Lizzie Collins' brick-and-tiled cottage perched preca-
riously on a roadside bank between the burnt cottages and
George Eyres' house. There was no room for even a
kitchen garden or a path around the back of the cottage,
though she did manage to squeeze in a flower border on
either side of the door. Lack of elbow-room outdoors was,
however, no hardship to Aunt Lizzie, who was a maiden
lady, sister to Reuben Collins of Box Cottage. Her later life
tended to be devoted to assisting in the upbringing of
proliferating great-nephews and nieces, but at the
beginning of the period of this survey she had already
achieved some celebrity as pig-killer's assistant. She was
the lady who on pig-killing day caught the blood in a
bucket and transformed it into black pudding.

On the opposite side of the road, tucked in against the
end of White Hill Farm, a brick-cob-and-slate cottage was
occupied by Granny Baugh. A very old lady, she was the
mother of Morris Baugh and Eva Clark, Will's wife.

Around the corner, by the lane known as The Green,
three pairs of cottages cowered under the ramparts of the
hill. Of the first two, one was occupied by Walt Collins
and his family in the early years of the story. After they
had departed for distant Norfolk in about 1920, behind
their threshing-machine, the cottage became home for a
succession of ephemeral workers, though for a time one or
two of Noah Whitlock's grandchildren lived there.

In a smaller adjoining cottage Harry Hurst and his wife Jane were spending their twilight years. Harry had spent much of his life as a drover, tramping the old droving tracks of England, and he loved to get an audience to listen to his tales down at the smithy on wet afternoons. In his old age his sight began to fail, and Jane walked with a decided limp. Both were decidedly thirsty characters.

The next site by The Green was occupied by a space, now gardens, where logically there should have been a house. And a house had indeed stood there until about thirty years earlier – the New Inn, kept by one Stephen Collins. It was remembered as a low, thatched building, with a skittle alley on the opposite side of the road. In a courtyard at the back was a well which served all the cottages in this corner of the village.

Carved out of the hillside at the back of the inn were the second pair of thatched cottages, each with two rooms up and two down and, of course, no back gardens. Access was by means of a long, steep path leading down to what was once the inn courtyard. In general these cottages changed occupants pretty frequently, as farmworkers came and went, but immediately after the war one of them was the home of the Stanhope family. Mr Charles Stanhope, an ex-soldier, was a London busdriver who emigrated to Wiltshire when motor transport began to offer a new range of jobs. Unhappily he died when his family of four girls and a boy were small, and a difficult task his widow had in rearing them, though she did it in the end quite triumphantly.

Just beyond the inn two other cottages still standing in 1911 were demolished soon afterwards. One was quickly replaced by a modern brick-and-slate house, which became a retirement home for a succession of elderly residents including, in the 1920s, Miss Pepper, the village schoolteacher. The other was never rebuilt but its foundations served for those of a barn.

Beyond these cottages the only houses on the south side of The Green, under the shadow of the hill, were Lot Whitlock's little farm and the rather similar cob-and-slate house next door. When the story begins, this was occupied by William Conduit and his wife, last members of an old Pitton family, of whom little is remembered. And this, according to repute, was as it should be, for The Green was said to have been a 'green way', thirty yards wide. During the centuries it had been narrowed by encroachment on the north or lower side but little affected to the south side, except for the planting of a couple of orchards.

On the lower side a series of cottages extended from one end of The Green to the other, beginning at the back of Ivyclad Farm. There, under a tall yew tree, a brick-cob-and-thatch cottage, with eaves drooping to within two feet off the ground, was in the early years occupied by Mr and Mrs Thomas Webb, brother to John. Later it happened to be empty at the time of the White Hill fire, so Mary Mills and her family were able to move into it.

Next came a chequerboard of gardens, now occupied by the residents of cottages nearby but owning, in part, their existence to the presence of another cottage now falling into ruin. Most of the gardens were cultivated by Morris Baugh, who lived in the nearer of a pair of cob-and-thatch cottages and who had a lean-to shed in which he trimmed thatching spars on wet days. Under a hedge on the opposite side of the road he usually kept a substantial pile of faggots around which he erected a rail fence, 'to keep the cows from hooking them about'. This tended to be gradually extended, illustrating how encroachment could begin and expand unless checked – which no one bothered to do.

The second of this pair of cottages was the traditional home of a family of Whites, the senior member of which was 'Aunt Maria', a little shrivelled old lady burdened with a set of dentures which didn't fit. Her deceased husband, Albert, was the brother of Noah of the Island Cottages, and cousin to Joshua White of Church Farm. A farmworker and a capable cornet-player in the village band, Albert was one of the first generation of villagers to take a look at London when the new railway made the journey feasible. When asked how he managed to make a living there, he mentioned various odd jobs he undertook, but added, 'Of course, I could always earn a bit, playing my cornet to the theatre queues.' His daughter Ada married Fred Kerley and had one son, Len, who became the village blacksmith. That is how the Kerleys came to Pitton, living in Albert's old cottage with his widow.

Leapfrogging Reg Eyres' farmyard brings us to two cob-and-thatch cottages crammed in at the top end of Abbot's Close. Each had miniscule gardens. One was generally occupied by a family of temporary farmworkers, but the other was for a number of years the home of George and Martha Noyce and their considerable family.

A narrow footpath, giving access to Abbots Close and known as 'The Drain' or 'The Drang', separated the Noyce cottage from a similar one which, like Mary Mills' cottage, featured overhanging thatched eaves falling almost to the ground and providing a covered work-space for Monday morning washtubs. It is dimly remembered that the resident in 1912 must have been old Eli Conduit, but afterwards it had a succession of occupants, nearly all temporary farmworkers.

Towards the far end of The Green, on the same side of the road, stood Aymer Cottage, presumably named after whoever gave his name to Aymer's Pond. It lay several feet below the level of the road and was a handsome though by no means spacious cob-and-thatch cottage, with its own well. Traditionally it belonged to one or another of the old village families. When the story begins, it was the home of Jesse and Jane Clark, parents of Will Clark of Webb's Farm. Later their daughter, who had married William Sheppard of Enford, came to live there.

At the very end of The Green, beyond which it degenerates into a footpath linking with Winterslow Hollow, stood a cob building which at various times served a number of purposes. Ted Whitlock remembered using it as a stable for his pony, Gyp. At another time, though whether before or after is impossible to say, it was called 'the Village Reading Room' and apparently served as a kind of club room for the young men of the village, who, from all accounts, indulged in plenty of horseplay on occasion. Either just before or just after the war it was transformed into a pleasant dwelling-house by a Mr Alfred Bell who had married into the Collins family and who came to Pitton to retire. Of his two sons, Reg, the elder, started the village bus service, which still flourishes. The younger, Eric, still living, was a highly talented artist and musician.

See how the same surnames keep cropping up. It used to be said that Pitton was a village of Whitlocks, Whites and Collinses, and such statistics as are available bear this out. In the 1851 census for the village, the first census which records the population in considerable detail, Pitton had 405 inhabitants, in 95 households. Of them 72 persons (19 households) bore the surname Whitlock, 46 (12 households) Collins, and 38 (8 households) White. Other fairly numerous clans were Fry, 26 persons in 6 households; Parsons, 18 persons in 6 households; and Cooke, 27 persons in 6 households.

The Whitlocks have been genealogically researched by a Family History Society – that popular modern study. They were resident in Pitton when the parish register starts, in 1605, and twenty-two Whitlock baptisms are recorded there between 1670 and 1700.

The 1851 Census reveals another remarkable fact. Out of the 405 persons then comprising the population, 313 were born in Pitton. The Clarendon estate accounted for 12 more, and of the rest 48 were born in adjacent villages, none more than 4 miles distant. Only 32 of the 405 inhabitants were born in more far-off places, such as Romsey, Salisbury and Dinton.

It was in 1826 that old William Cobbett encountered in a village not far north of Andover a young woman who had never been more than three miles from her home. At that date her record could probably have been matched by dozens of Pitton's inhabitants.

Such was the village, this community of then approximately 300 souls, just before the outbreak of the First World War. As a record some of the details are lacking, for, as this chronicle is being prepared in 1987, 1912 is on the very fringe of human memory. In the respect that Pitton was virtually classless, it was a remarkable entity. Some of the farmers had graduated from families of agricultural labourers, and some of the labourers had near relations who were farmers. The absence of a resident squire and parson doubtless assisted this levelling, and certainly there was little difference in financial status between master and men. All were poor and had such long experience of poverty that for them it was entirely normal. Life consisted of days of hard labour against the familiar pageant of the seasons, and efforts which were frustrated by fickle or downright hostile weather. That had always been the lot of the peasants.

As can readily be imagined, the village was a microcosm of the world at large. Virtually all human life was here. Birth, marriage and death (the last still announced by the passing bell) were familiar events. So were the carrying-ons of young people and the arrival of illegitimate babies. Men were unfaithful to their wives, wives to their husbands. Wives were ill-treated, husbands were hen-pecked. Feuds flourished, and there are memories of fights, with women tearing out each other's hair on the public highway. Among the 300 or so souls were greedy characters, grasping characters, pig-headed characters (numerous these!), saintly characters, rakes, misers, cheats, grumpy curmudgeons, laughing humorists. All were well known to their neighbours, their little foibles and weaknesses thoroughly discussed by the village gossips.

When the war was at last over and life was settling back into its old ruts, some changes had taken place. Time had taken its normal harvest of the old, resulting in a considerable swopping of residences. The death toll included Mrs Mark Collins, Mr and Mrs Abram Talbot, Mrs Downer, Joby Compton, Noah Whitlock, Noah White, Mr Legge, Arthur White, Mr and Mrs Stephen Seward, Jim Fry, George Noyce, George Eyres, John Webb, Mr and Mrs Jesse Clark, Lot Whitlock and probably a few others – memory is dim. Possibly some of these survived a little longer; a memorial in the chapel to John Webb records that he died in 1920.

Most of the men came home from the war and settled

down as though they had never been away. In the realities of life for them, the fields of Old Lawn and Church Living, the lanes of Cockroad and Slateway, the yew trees of Monkey's Castle and the old beech with its burden of carved initials at the entrance to Hunts Copse were far more significant than the plains of Mesopotamia and the trenches of Flanders.

The ex-soldier Ernest Whitlock and his brother-in-law Walter White took over Lodge Farm. Sid, Ernest's brother, became roadman in John Webb's place. A new generation of boys and girls began (and in many instances finished) their education at Pitton school. And the scene was set for a new era in which they were supposed to play a dominant part.

It was an age of optimism. This generation was reared on the promises of the 'war to end wars' and the League of Nations. It was fed and nurtured by *The Children's Newspaper*. Progress was the keynote. Everything was going to improve and keep on improving. Even materially and financially the prospects seemed good. Farm wages had risen to thirty shillings a week, and the prices of farm produce were stabilized by the Corn Production Act. Even for the very poor the workhouse bread-van had become a fading memory, for the introduction of the old-age pension in 1910 had to some extent banished the shadow of the workhouse and provided a modicum of support for the elderly in their own homes.

True, water still had to be hauled manually by bucket and windlass from deep wells. The village was still regularly cut off from the outside world once or twice in most winters. Oil lamps, lanterns and candles were the only sources of illumination. No one yet possessed a car, though some villagers had seen one. The major treat of the year, at least for women and children, was the Sunday School outing, by farm waggon, to a destination never more than six or eight miles away.

Still, things were looking up. People felt that they were entitled to progress after all the sacrifices of the Great War, and they thought they detected ample evidence that they were going to be rewarded.

What, one might ask, is the most remarkable feature of this survey of a typical but unremarkable village? Surely the fact that such an in-depth survey is possible after a lapse of nearly seventy years. An atmosphere of permanence pervades the scene. The comings and goings of a minority of temporary farmworkers are set against the immobility of a community of families which had been rooted there for centuries. Children of the 1910s and 1920s grew up against a background in which every feature, down to individual bushes, gates, paths and apple trees, not only was familiar to themselves but had also been familiar to their parents and grandparents when they were young.

The author and his cousin Mark were reminiscing about their boyhood days. Old Sergeant, the horse on Mark's father's farm, was mentioned.

'I used to go over and rack en up at nights.' said Mark, 'and there was always the cat curled up in the manger. Old Spot. You minds Old Spot surely?'

And, oddly enough, he did remember Old Spot, after nearly sixty-five years.

An innovation thought to have resulted from the 1912 Sale was the establishing of a few acres of land on the south side of Bottom Way as allotments. Villagers could rent plots there for a few shillings a year, and during the 1920s and 1930s many of them did so, cycling there from the village on spring and summer evenings, their digging forks tied to the handle-bars.

'Where be gwaine then you?'

'Oh, out the 'llotments.'

The custom gradually declined, however, and eventually died with the war.

Although Pitton is not good apple-growing territory, the stratum of soil over the chalk being too shallow, the village formerly possessed many more orchards than it does now or did even in the 1920s and 1930s. At the turn of the century there were no fewer than four portable

7   Roads and Transport

The topography of Pitton is easy to understand. The village is a compact, nucleated unit as dictated by its situation on the floor of a normally waterless downland valley. The map shows how four roads cross at right angles in the middle of the village. The north-west road, Whiteway, leads to the London Road (now the A30) and so to Salisbury; the north-east, Bottom Way, to Winterslow; the south-east, White Hill, up over the hill to Farley; the south-west, Slateway, to the Clarendon estate.

However, research suggests that this is an over-simplification. Whiteway apparently lost itself on the downs in the days before enclosure, as soon as it crossed the boundary from Pitton parish into Winterbourne. When the downs were open, uncultivated and unfenced, it had a number of alternative routes to choose from and was, in any case, not much used.

Somewhat similarly, Bottom Way was largely a creation of the enclosure of 1819. The old road to Winterslow took a turn to the right one field beyond the north end of the village, up the hill still known as Winterslow Hollow. Even in the 1920s Winterslow Hollow was officially maintained as the main link between the two villages. The importance of Bottom Way at and after the enclosure is intimately linked with rise of the Pheasant Inn (Winterslow Hutt, in those days) as a coaching stage. Here horses were changed, and travellers took the opportunity to stretch their legs and sample the local ale. And hither came the men of Pitton and Winterslow after the day's work was done, to meet, drink and hear the latest news from distant London. Bottom Way was, however, no more than a muddy cart track at a time when Winterslow Hollow was metalled – at least with flints.

The road to Farley was excessively meandering. It started by winding its way up White Hill necessarily, for the gradient was one in nine – and continued between hedge-crossed banks down the long incline to Farley village. The section from the top of the hill to Farley was known to the Pitton people as Farley Lane, to the Farley people as Pitton Road.

From 1874 onwards Farley and Pitton formed one parish, as already noted, but before that they were chapelries of Alderbury – a somewhat larger village, some three or four miles to the south-west, on the banks of the Avon. Alderbury was thus the parent of both villages, a state of affairs deep-rooted in history.

Pitton's links with Alderbury were considerable, and much traffic must have passed between the two villages in medieval times. It did not, however, follow the present detour via Farley or take short cuts through the forest. Instead it carved out a winding but evidently venerable route, rutted well below the level of the surrounding fields, which skirted the edge of the park. From Pitton village this route was the straight section of road known as Slateway. At the end of the lane one branch, probably of comparatively recent date, swerved right to the park entrance known as Pitton Gate. The left fork proceeded to climb the scarp by a steep, winding way known as Dunley Hill. At the top it bore right again and wandered, by a tortuous sunken way very similar to Farley Lane, downhill to Hunt's Copse, a detached coppice of Clarendon, and so, by the way of another hill called Sat Hill and an ancient way known as Lucewood (locally 'Luce-ood') Lane, to Alderbury. The lane itself bore the name of Cockroad. As Dunley Hill was extremely steep, much traffic preferred the still trying gradient of White Hill, at the top of which a link lane to the right joined up at the top of Dunley. All these lanes were kept in repair by the Pitton roadman until the county council undertook responsibility for the highways in 1928. Then it was arbitrarily decided that Slateway should still be a charge on the county exchequer, doubtless because it gave access to important Clarendon House, but that Dunley and Cockroad should be abandoned. They are still narrow cobbled lanes, used mostly by tractors and horses but pleasant green ways in summer.

Another hard road, kept in repair by the roadman until 1928, turned sharply to the left at the top of White Hill. After a course of a few hundred yards the roadman's responsibilities ended, but the track, green and rutted, continued through the fields, linking up eventually with Winterslow Hollow. Dirty Lane was the appropriate local name for it. At the point when the flint road ended and the ruts began, another narrow lane, known as Green Lane, bore off to the right at right angles, to end eventually in a cul-de-sac. Farther on, yet another green lane ran parallel to Green Lane on an extended course which took it to the edge of Farley Copse and so, through the woods, to Farley village.

This grid pattern of lanes on the southern slopes of the hill had their origin deep in history, for they seem to be intimately linked with the 'Ancient Enclosures' marked on the 1819 map. Even in 1912 much of the land was still divided into one-acre fields, divided by wide hedges, as already described. By that date most of them had become amalgamated into one farm, Webb's Farm, but a few belonged to other owners.

On the principle that in a thirty-yard stretch of hedgerow the number of species of bush or tree is a rough though reliable guide, in centuries, to the age of the hedge, these 'Ancient Enclosures' were probably made about AD 1200. There were and are about seven well-established species, namely hawthorn, blackthorn, hazel, holly, oak, maple, wayfaring-tree, dog-rose. By way of contrast, the hedges by Bottom Way were almost purely of hawthorn, though some elder, brambles and dog-roses were beginning to establish themselves. These hedges were obviously planted in or soon after 1819.

The 1819 enclosures had carved up the Bottom Way fields so neatly into rectangles that only one subsidiary lane was required – The Drove, an excessively muddy track giving access to the top fields. Each farmer, however, made his own cart-tracks.

Back in the village itself, several minor lanes were graced with names. The Green, already noted, seems to have been an ancient through-way of considerable breadth, the footpath known as Cold Harbour being a continuation of it.

Parallel to the Street, on the other or northern side of the valley, a short lane called Bove Hedges linked Whiteway with Manor Farm. The name is of considerable antiquity, denoting a time when hedges were to be found only around the village houses and home pastures. This land ran 'above the hedges'.

Joining it at right angles by Manor Farm, Black Lane is supposed to have a recent derivation. In 1863 or 1864 a horrendous conflagration, said to have been started by boys playing in a barn, destroyed two farms, several cottages and umpteen barns and other farm buildings. Black Lane apparently refers to the blackened ruins. The two farmers concerned, one a young man named Maton, were so discouraged that they emigrated to Australia. The Island Cottages, already mentioned, were said to have been built to house some of the workers who had lost their homes.

Church Lane's deviation is obvious. It is the lane which leads to the church and then dives to the left to join Black Lane.

Important as all these roads and lanes were in the life of the village, they were not more so than the footpaths. Roads and tracks were for carts and waggons; paths were for pedestrians. Most important of all was the footpath through Clarendon Woods to Salisbury. As it led directly to King Manor, the site of the royal palace, it could well have been older than the city of Salisbury itself. No one without a vehicle would ever have thought of going to or from Salisbury by road. For one thing, the path cut nearly two miles off the journey.

At some time earlier in the twentieth century, an owner of the Clarendon estate attempted to stop the villagers of Pitton and Farley using the estate paths. The villagers were indignant, and a court case ensued. All the old men and women, dressed in their Sunday best, were escorted to Devizes to testify that they had used the paths ever since they could remember. The result was a compromise. The parishioners were no longer able to wander at will through the woods but were confirmed in their rights to use two paths, one from Pitton to Salisbury and one from Farley to Salisbury. By the 1920s, as motor transport became general, the paths lost some of their old significance, though many villagers still cycled along them regularly. Now they make a pleasant afternoon ramble in summer.

Access to the Pitton path through Clarendon was by way of a footpath, known as Pitton Stile, at the back of Parsonage Farm and over Parsonage Farm fields, thence along the edge of the woods to the forest houses known as Four Cottages. The path was equally important to the people of Winterslow, whose direct way to Salisbury lay through Pitton. Old residents used to relate that a constant procession of pedestrians could be seen tramping over the fields to the woods on Tuesday and Saturday mornings (market days) and back in the evenings. The

Winterslow people had their route marked out to a nicety, to save any unnecessary steps. Invariably they came down Winterslow Hollow to its junction with The Green, then along The Green, down Abbots' Close and by way of Church Lane, Black Lane and Bove Hedges to Parsonage Farm.

Some of the pedestrians burdened themselves with heavy loads. An old market woman from Winterslow used to walk to Salisbury, laden with eggs, poultry, butter and other farm produce, twice a week and return with all kinds of commodities purchased on request for village customers. Arthur Whitlock said that he once tried to estimate the weight of her load and found he could hardly lift it. It must have been well over a half-hundredweight, was his opinion. She and several other traders did a good trade in fresh fish at certain seasons.

Of other footpaths, Cold Harbour existed, of course, to serve the three cottages at the far end. According to etymologists, Cold Harbour, a common place-name on English maps, should refer to a Roman ruin, where, in later ages, a benighted traveller could find comfortless lodgings. No such Roman site is known near this Cold Harbour, though one may possibly await discovery, but the name may have migrated a half-mile or so from the Roman shrine by Nemett's Lane (see p.20). Beyond Cold Harbour cottages other footpaths linked up with Slateway, Dunley Hill and Cockroad, and there was one, long disused, which evidently served as a short cut to Farley Lane for cottagers thirsty for a drink at Farley's pub, the Hook and Glove.

The track already mentioned, from the bottom end of Dirty Lane to Farley Copse, was also in frequent use as a footpath from Pitton to Farley, again by thirsty workers making as near as possible a bee-line for the Hook and Glove. From Pitton village it was served by two paths over the crest of the hill, one from the vicinity of the former New Inn and one directly from the footpath through Abbots' Close.

This list of footpaths is the one which found its place in the early parish maps, but in essence it was temporary. It recorded the paths then in use, and they were in use simply because they served the purpose of linking as directly as possible two fixed points, normally a workman's cottage and his favourite glass of ale. The worker went as straight as possible for his goal, regardless of whose property he was crossing. When he died or moved house or became infirm or a teetotaller, the path died too. There was no permanency about it, any more than there was for the tracks over the unfenced downs.

The new era of motor traffic opened the doors to a wider horizon too late for many of the older generation to appreciate it.

One day in the early 1920s some of old Noah White's younger relations decided to take him and his wife Rachel on an excursion to Bournemouth, to see the sea for the very first time. They sat the old couple in deckchairs on the sand, facing the sea, for a few hours.

What were their impressions? No one seemed to know. Noah and Rachel had no words to describe their feelings. Later, in his pocket account book, Noah recorded the event:

'Noah White and Rachel White went to Bourne Mouth September 6, 1922, and Miss E Fry and Mrs Harland and Miss S Harland, Mr Edwin Whitlock and Mrs E Whitlock And Ther 3 Chilren and Miss Kate Whitlock, and Mr Edwin Whitlock's sister.'

That was all. It was important enough to be one of the few events recorded in his notebook, but what it meant to him was beyond his power to express. Perhaps not very much. He was too old, and the experience was so far beyond his normal range.

Ted Whitlock recalled that an eccentric Winterslow character, Monty Paler, when offered a lift home in a pony and trap, replied, 'Can't stop now. I'm in a hurry!'

That was not quite as stupid as it may sound to us, for Monty was simply confusing the pony and trap with the carrier's cart, of which he had had experience. And it was certainly quicker to walk than to travel by carrier's cart. A covered waggon with a black tilt, it was drawn by an aged horse, too decrepit for farm work, and needed 2½ hours to cover the six miles to town. The author who remembers making the journey as a very small boy, recalls excited comment when, from the top of Joyner's Hill, the passengers would cry, 'I can see the telegraph wires!' The passengers were nearly all old men, handicapped people and mothers with children; everyone else found it quicker to walk. It was normal for everyone able to do so to alight at the bottom of steep Joyner's Hill and walk, to lighten the load for the horse. Sometimes, when the road was in a very bad condition, it was necessary to help by pushing the vehicle.

Tuesdays and Saturdays (market days in Salisbury) were the days for the carrier's cart, and usually the chief business of the carrier was with freight and parcels. The carrier was used to taking notes from housewives to the Salisbury tradesmen, even for intimate items such as chemises and corsets. Each carrier from the scores of villages around Salisbury had his traditional depot at a Salisbury pub, so that tradesmen would know where to deliver parcels for a particular village. Pitton's depot was the William IV in Milford Street.

A tragic tale is told of how Daniel Whitlock collapsed with an epileptic fit in a Salisbury Street. Passers-by forced a drink of brandy into him and, someone recognizing him as a Pitton man, they carried him to the William IV and dumped him in the carrier's cart. In due course the carrier arrived and, smelling the brandy, assumed he had a drunk to deal with and unconcernedly set off for home. Arriving at the corner in the middle of the village, he and the other passengers hauled Daniel out of the cart and laid him on the roadside grass. Someone went to advise his wife Jane of the situation.

Now Daniel had had a somewhat chequered life-story so far. Apparently he had been a typically wild harum-scarum in his youth but was now settling down to married life. It was a period when Victorian teetotalism was at its peak, and Jane, who had been in service in London, was affected. A 'born-again' Christian, she had worked vigorously on Daniel, until he too became converted and foreswore the demon drink. Hurrying down to the corner, she found her husband lying on the grass in apparently a drunken stupor. Sickened and mortified, she turned on her heel and left him there. Some time later he recovered consciousness and managed to stagger up the road and upstairs to bed. But the attack and the long exposure had taken their toll, and he never got up again. Jane was left a widow, to rear three small children on parish relief.

The village was split in apportioning the blame for what had happened. Jane never wavered in her belief that drink had killed her husband, but many other villagers appreciated the true state of affairs. The youngest of Jane's children, Ted, was six months old at the time. In later life he sometimes asked people about the mystery behind his father's death but always met with the evasive answer, 'You'd better ask your mother.' He died at the age of eighty-nine, never knowing the truth.

When, in his speech on the occasion of the tree-planting to commemorate King George V's Jubilee in 1935, Owen Griffin said, 'No previous generation has ever seen such changes as we have seen,' he had in mind primarily the changes in transport. It was as though the forces that restricted the horizons of the village had been suddenly thrown down and the wide world lay open to whoever chose to step out into it. The carrier's cart made its last journey in the early 1920s, and in its place the motor car arrived.

Several villagers still living can remember seeing the first car ever to enter the village and the first aeroplane to fly over it, but Ted Whitlock, who died in 1967 aged eighty-nine, claimed to have been the first person in the village to own a bicycle. He meant, of course, a bicycle of conventional type, for it was remembered that some years earlier a Pitton man, believed to have been Jim Fry, acquired a penny-farthing bicycle, with solid rubber tyres, and rode to Southampton on it – a journey of twenty-one miles! Ted bought his bicycle when he was a member of the Pitton shearing gang and was henceforward given the job of going ahead to the next farm to advise them of the gang's impending arrival.

Alfred Bell possessed the first car to be owned by a Pitton resident, but soon the movement to mechanized transport snowballed. Lewis White pensioned off his old carrier's cart, and his son Lionel acquired a commercial vehicle which could serve as a bus, lorry or cattle cart. Reg Bell set up business as a bus proprietor, announcing a regular timetable of services to Salisbury. At least, it was supposed to be regular, but the early buses were decidedly temperamental, especially when starting in the morning. Reg's bus was a solid-tyred Panhard, which he kept in a shed in Owen Griffin's yard at Parsonage Farm. As they assembled for morning school, the children used to line the playground to watch a succession of stalwart 'experts' swinging the starting handle till the sweat poured off them and bad language out of them. The schoolmistress would come hurrying out to shepherd her charges inside, away from contamination.

In 1921 Ted Whitlock bought a one-ton Ford van that had been built in America for use in France but arrived there too late to see active service. It had, of course, a left-hand drive, though it was equipped with the new pneumatic tyres. There were no real gears, as a modern driver would understand them. When the engine began to labour too poignantly uphill, the driver had to press hard on a pedal with his left foot – and hold it there. The engine then ran in low gear. A long hill was a testing ordeal, not so much for the car's engine as for the driver's endurance. The exhaust pipe just under the floorboards could be seen glowing red-hot. If eventually he weakened and lifted his foot, the engine stopped – and when it would start again was anybody's guess. Self-starters were, of course, refinements of the future. Ideally one man swung the starting-handle while another sat in the driver's seat and manipulated the levers, one of which was the accelerator and the other controlled the rate of sparking.

It can be said that the younger men of the village took to motor vehicles like proverbial ducks to water. They not only learned quickly how to drive them but had to discover how they worked. Motors were stripped and put together again, and tea-table conversation was soon featuring sparking plugs, carburettors, distributors and other technical terms which would have been incomprehensible to an earlier generation. The smithy loomed large in the new revolution, for the early cars were solidly built vehicles, of a type for which a competent blacksmith could readily make spare parts. In a back street of Salisbury a firm actually began making cars of its own design – Scout cars. The enterprise flourished for a time but could not cope with the fierce competition which developed.

With the new motor transport, the urgent need to improve the roads became self-evident. The cobbled streets of the towns and the muddy tracks of the countryside were just adequate for horses and carts but hopelessly inefficient for cars. John Webb, and Sid Whitlock after him, could manage to keep the Pitton roads in their accustomed state of repair under the old regime, but the task soon became too much for one man.

Roads, it was accepted, should be made of local stone, and the only local stone in or around Pitton was flint. Ploughing and cultivating brought a new crop of small flints to the surface of the arable fields every few years, and they were then harvested by stone-pickers, generally old men and women. The stone-pickers quartered each field, picking up the stones by hand into buckets and being paid contract rates – so much a cubic yard. Long experience made stone-pickers and their customers expert at estimating a cubic yard – or just a yard, as it was termed: so many bucketfuls per heap, and so many heaps per cart load. The cartloads were then deposited in long, sloping heaps by the roadsides, where they would be used, and paid for, by the parish council. The roadman tapped the heaps as he needed, using the flints for filling in pot-holes and ruts.

The wear on road surface was considerable, not only because all cart and waggon wheels were iron-bonded and cut deep ruts but also because the foundation of the roads was of chalk, which in the thaw after hard winter frost deteriorated into a gooey white paste. In those circumstances roads quickly became impassable, especially on hills. Whiteway and White Hill were regularly in trouble, but villagers still living can remember occasions when Three-Mile Hill, on the main Salisbury-London road, was likewise blocked.

With the coming of motor traffic, the age-old system whereby a parish was responsible for the upkeep of its roads was plainly inadequate, and in 1928 the onus was shifted to the county council. Granite and chippings arrived to replace the local flints, and a steam-roller consolidated them into a surface better than the village had ever known – equal, in fact, to that of city streets. The villagers commented on that very fact!

'Lumme!' they said. 'We shall be havin' street lighting next!'

There was a price to pay, though. The county council did not accept their new responsibilities without question. They got busy with their pruning shears. Certain roads were declared redundant and erased from the list for which the council accepted responsibility. They included Cockroad, Dirty Lane and Winterslow Hollow. The new arrangement meant that now vehicles had to travel to Winterslow via Bottom Way and to Alderbury via Farley, detours which formerly they would never have dreamed of making.

For the time being, however, the council retained the village roadman on the old basis. He was now responsible to the council supervisor instead of to the parish council but for most of the time carried on much as usual. Only after the steam-roller appeared was he one of a gang. This arrangement lasted until well after the 1939-45 war.

If the younger men of the village took instinctively to the internal combustion engine, the same could hardly be said of the older generation. They regarded the motor car with suspicion and misgivings. How it worked was a mystery beyond their comprehension. Their attitude was accurately conveyed in a book very popular in the West Country at that time, *Old Biskit*, written in the Devon dialect by Jan Stewer (A.J.Coles). 'Old Biskit', his car, had a personality and will of its own, which Jan strove in vain to master. What went on under its bonnet was as much of a mystery to him as what went on under his wife's bonnet. As for the intricacies of putting the car into reverse, the best that Jan could do by way of explanation was, 'I don't rightly know how it happens, but when you touches thik reverse lever, it causeth all the innerds to dap round backurds.'

Few of the older men were bold enough to venture behind the wheel of a car, but when tractors appeared some of them felt they had to move with the times. Men working on the neighbouring fields used to be amused at the reactions of Bill Keel, who talked to his tractor as he would to his horses.

'Gee! Gee! Wug off, there! Wug off! Hi-step now! Whoa! Whoa! I say! WAY!'

And when the tractor laboured going uphill, Bill could be seen heaving forward giving great pushes with his body as he urged the machine on.

That was quite late in our story, though – towards the end of the 1930s. Ted Whitlock bought the first tractor to come to Pitton, and that was in 1934. It was a second-hand Ford with iron wheels and strakes. To take it on the roads, the blacksmith manufactured some road bands to fit over the strakes, but fitting them on and taking them off again took so long that it was hardly worth the trouble.

In the 1920s there was some controversy about the type of car for the future. Would it be the open car with detachable side-screens and a folding top or the newer saloon type? The open car was first in favour, and it lingered longest in the charabancs which before long replaced the farm waggon as the vehicle for excursions and outings. Photographs of those early outings, usually to Bournemouth, depict open charabancs crowded with happy people, many of them eating fish and chips.

The village bus services, run by Reg Bell and Lionel White in competition, though Lionel White was soon specializing in freight, did not aspire to charabancs. Buses were, however, sometimes pressed into service for excursions, and the memory of what must have been one of the earliest traffic jams in history caused by motor vehicles is still green.

The Outing was to Bournemouth, and the bus was packed with cheerful excursionists, who sat on hard seats facing each other along the inner walls but whose leg space was cramped by additional cross-seating, consisting of planks, which had been fitted in to cope with overbooking. The bus was closed in, not open, and had a roof-rack for luggage, in everyday use for taking awkwardly shaped items to market. Riding inside was so uncomfortable that all the able-bodied chaps clambered up and sat on the roof-rack. And so they set out on the thirty-mile journey to Bournemouth.

There are few if any hills worthy of the name on the journey down the Avon valley, but by the time the over-laden bus reached Christchurch it was panting with exhaustion. And on a narrow, hump-backed stone bridge over the Avon it gave up the struggle and shuddered to a halt. The driver inspected the engine, which appeared to be over-heated.

'It wants some more water in the radiator,' was the opinion of one self-styled expert, and there, ready to hand, was plenty of water, under the bridge.

So the driver unscrewed the radiator cap – with predictable results. A fountain of scalding water spurted aloft, spraying not only the driver but the lads on the roof-rack. Never was a site evacuated with greater speed. Numbering more than a dozen, they dived over the sides and came tumbling down, to the bewilderment of the inside passengers.

The bus stuck on the bridge for well over an hour, holding up a long tail of traffic on the approach road on either side, for the nearest alternative route was via Ringwood, ten miles away. It was well after mid-day before the outing arrived at its destination, Bournemouth Square. Time to go in search of food, except for those, the majority, who had brought sandwiches. At one o'clock it started to rain, and for the rest of the afternoon most of the excursionists huddled under Bournemouth pier, sheltering from a grey, unceasing downpour. The organizers expressed disillusionment with sea-side holidays.

'Give me the old days when we went by waggon to Amesbury,' they lamented. 'At least there was a barn we could get into.'

8 Water

One of the most important items in Saturday's preparation for the Sabbath was the drawing of water by windlass from the village wells. Conventionally that was the responsibility of the man of the household on Saturday afternoons or evenings. Pulling up a ten-gallon bucket of water from a depth of eighty feet occupied, say, ten minutes, so most householders had to reckon on an hour or two's work at the end of the week, except, of course, when providential rain relieved them of the chore. Rainwater was, of course, perfectly satisfactory for washing, though hardly for drinking (unless boiled). Drinking water was stored in large earthenware pans, generally fitted with a lid.

Drawing water on a Sunday was naturally taboo and, of course, it was impossible to transgress surreptitiously, for the sound of a bucket hurtling down a well was unmistakable. Even the most irreligious villager would not flout convention to that extent.

In times of drought drawing water was a major preoccupation for farmers, who had to employ a man virtually full-time to supply the needs of the farm livestock. Lewis Parsons, mentally handicapped to the extent that he was illiterate, often spent much of the summer at this task. Some farmers possessed a well-bucket consisting of two buckets welded or riveted together at the lip. This doubled its carrying capacity but made the work that much harder.

Every farm had its own well, as did some of the better houses and cottages, but several workers' cottages usually had to share a well. The well at White Hill Farm (at 120 feet the deepest in the village) served all the cottages around that corner, under the dust-cloud of the lime-kilns. At one time that meant twelve or fifteen cottages, which had to operate a rota. The well was on White Hill Farm property, thus belonging to Ted Whitlock, who was expected to keep the well-crib in repair and provide bucket and rope. The other householders paid him a shilling a year for the privilege of using the well.

Every now and again a party of gypsies would camp for a few days on the green at the top of White Hill, making pegs from hazel-rods filched from neighbouring hedges, and invariably they would come to the door of White Hill Farm with the request, 'Can we use your well, mister?' The request was usually granted – it wasn't wise to make enemies of gypsies – but time and again, through lack of skill, they would fail to apply the brake when the bucket hit the water. The rope then unwound itself from the windlass, broke away and careered to the bottom of the well, whereupon the gypsies vanished, leaving the fuming householders to retrieve the rope and bucket with grappling-irons (blacksmith-made), a time-consuming task which also tended to foul the water.

Surviving villagers who remember that era can locate the sites of wells, nearly all of which have now been filled in. As new houses have been built, however, subsidences have revealed other wells in forgotten places. One was discovered during the 1921 drought, when subsidence caused a cob wall that had been subsequently built over an inadequately filled well to collapse. This wall enclosed a garden by the central corner of the village, a garden which appeared to be that of a vanished house.

There was some speculation that it may have marked the precincts of the original village inn. As the pub by The Green was called the New Inn, the natural inference was that there must have been an older inn, and what more likely site than the village crossroads? The theory was strengthened by the discovery, in the garden, in the 1920s of a wine-bottle seal bearing the date 1637.

Where the top end of the garden adjoined Webb's Farm, Moses Webb in the eighteenth century had a little smithy, where he made the weathercock that still adorns St Peter's Church; perhaps he also shod the horses of travellers who stopped at the village inn.

The other primary source of water in this normally dry valley was a pond. Aymers Pond, the village pond, has already been noted. It presumably belonged to the parish but apparently required next to no maintenance. In addition, most of the farmers possessed their own pond. The exception was White Hill Farm, which, as noted, had graduated from cottage to farm status in the current century and, because of its situation, had had no chance to acquire this traditional water supply.

The conventional arrangement was for the pond to be situated in the middle of the farmyard, allowing rainwater from the roofs of farmhouse and barns to drain into it. It was also handy for the use of the farm horses and other housed livestock. The arrangement proved reasonably satisfactory for as long as the farm livestock consisted chiefly of sheep, which seldom came into the farmyard, but it failed disastrously when the sheep were replaced by cows, which came into the buildings twice a day for milking. For several hours before and after milking they stood around in the yard, fouling the water as they drank. To make matters worse, the bedding required by the cows when housed in winter produced huge quantities of farmyard manure which, when removed from the cattle pens, was piled in oozing heaps in the yard, often at the edge of the pond, waiting to be carted to the fields. Apart from general hygiene (a word unknown to that generation!), the spread of any infectious cattle disease, such as Johne's Disease, was inevitable.

Three of the village farms – namely, Church Farm, Cold Harbour Farm and Parsonage Farm – had in times past constructed ponds in certain meadows, so that cows could drink without having to use the highway. Even these ponds, however, dried up in dry summers. Their problem was that, like most chalkland ponds, they had been constructed for sheep, which required less drinking-water than cows. Also, while dainty hooves of sheep tended to consolidate rather than damage the bottom of ponds, the heavier and clumsier hooves of cattle wore holes in it. Whether the art had been forgotten locally or whether the financial depression of the 1920s and 1930s made the operation impossible, no one now living remembers ever seeing the village ponds cleaned or renovated.

A system of roadside ditches, with occasional drains beneath the road, carried rainwater down the steep White Hill to ponds at the bottom. Old Nathaniel Betteridge, who once lived at White Hill Cottage, diverted some of it to feed a tiny duck-pond he made in his garden, but most of the drainage careered on down the hill to finish up in the yard pond at Webb's Farm. From there the overflow streamed across the road and into another ditch which carried it into the meadow pond of Cold Harbour Farm. Ted Whitlock was exercised about the effect of the county council's road-building operations after 1928, which progressively raised the road level. New ditches took the White Hill water straight into the meadow pond but, 'What's going to happen to the overflow from Webb's Farm pond?' he demanded, 'It'll be all bayed back here.'

The County Surveyor was unimpressed, pointing out that the overflow was, in any case, mostly urine.

Incidentally, the road surfaces are now several inches above their levels of sixty years ago. One steps *down* from the Bottom Way road onto the muddy verges, for instance, whereas previously one stepped down from the grass verges onto the muddy road.

The village ponds were in demand for one other purpose. The visiting threshing-machine was powered by a steam-engine which needed frequent refilling with water. The threshing-machine driver had to plan his route from village to village carefully, to ensure that he did not run short of water on his journeys. Each farm was required to supply enough water to take the machine to the next watering-place, which could create problems in a dry autumn or frozen winter. Ponds were the obvious source of supply, for no one relished the prospect of drawing sufficient well-water to fill a steam-engine boiler.

One other aspect of water supply has to be mentioned. Pitton lies in a valley possessing that peculiarity of the chalk country, a winterbourne. In autumn and winter the water table in the chalk sometimes rises sufficiently to break through the surface and form a temporary stream. In many downland valleys this happens every year, but the Pitton valley is situated at the very headwaters of its stream, which flows through Clarendon, East Grimstead and West Dean to find its way eventually into the River Test and so to Southampton Water.

A record kept in the first part of the present century until the 1950s shows that 'the springs', as they were called, produced a winterbourne on average about once in seven years. Noah White, underwood worker, who died in, it is thought, 1924, jotted down in one of his account books dates on which the springs started flowing through Pitton. They are: 19 January 1873, 25 January 1877, 16 February 1883, 13 February 1904, 31 January 1913, 19 January 1915, 31 March 1919. The idea that the phenomenon occurred about once in seven years is thus seen as an average.

'The springs' were a notable feature in village life. In the well at Box Cottage, where at the beginning of this story Reuben Collins lived, a stone was eagerly watched as the danger point neared.

When the water reaches the black stone,
The springs will break out in Old Lawn.

Whether the couplet has any antiquity or whether it is a
fairly recent concoction by local lads, the observation was
accurate. Within a few days of their appearing in Old
Lawn, the springs formed a stream which began to flow
through the village. Unfortunately there was no proper
channel for the water for most of the course. It spread in
great shallow pools over farmland and gardens. Some
cottages even had springs bubbling up through the beaten
earth floors, causing the housewife to roll up the
coco-matting. In the Bakery a spring actually rose under
Aunt Polly's fireplace.

Through the village itself a ditch, though quite
inadequate, carried off some of the water, and a brick
bridge had been built to take the Salisbury road over it.
The ditch had been dug at some time soon after the
middle of the nineteenth century when an epidemic,
thought (probably correctly) to be connected with the
pools of stagnant water, swept the village one May,
causing alarming casualties. Old William Baugh said that
at one time three of his sisters were lying dead together in
the front room of their cottage (on the site of the present
Cherry Tree Cottage).

A new schoolmistress who arrived one year after the
Christmas holidays got herself and her pupils thoroughly
confused when she asked them whether their village
possessed a river. They didn't know.

'Come now, what's that water flowing under the
bridge?'

'That idden a river, miss. That's the springs!'

To the children, accustomed to life in a normally
waterless village, the springs were a god-send. Many of
them could not get farther than their front door without
paddling. The family living in Willow Cottage had to
emerge through the garden of Church House and then
proceed by way of Black Lane and Bove Hedges if they
wanted to get to the shop or to chapel. As for the church,
it was closed for the duration, the cellar being deep in

water. The springs meandered along the valley, crossed the road at Dunstable and Bentley Farm and, in the village, flooded the road by Aymers Pond, the Bakery and along the Street as far as Box Cottage.

Memories linger of barn doors being taken off hinges and used as rafts or punts and soakings in consequence; also of strange birds, such as moorhens and redshanks, never seen here normally, suddenly appearing and remaining to nest.

The springs normally broke in November or December but sometimes not until after Christmas. Local wisdom associated their rising with the wind direction.

'Ah, the wind bin down the south-west for more'n a wik. We shall soon have the springs down.'

In fact, the observation, though correct, was probably due to the south-west wind bringing ample rain. The floods were at their height in early March, and the last pools usually dried up in early May. Cereal crops in flooded fields were a write-off, but farmers could use the land for catch-crops of turnips or kale.

More than twenty years have now elapsed since the springs last broke in Pitton. The water-table in the chalk has evidently been sinking steadily. New residents tend to be sceptical about the tales of floods, and it *is* difficult to believe in them.

The senior citizens who remember them well regard wet summers and wetter autumns with hopeful anticipation: 'I hope I live long enough to see the springs down just once more!' they say. It would, they feel, be a just nemesis falling on those who have ignored their advice and built new houses on sites which were once flooded regularly.

But the years pass and the springs stay well below the surface. It is unlikely that they will be seen again.

9 Church, Chapel and School

The saying 'as different as chalk from cheese' originates in Wiltshire. It refers to the remarkable contrast between the two unequal divisions of the county. Two-thirds of Wiltshire consists of undulating chalk downs; the other third, in the north-west, is of rich valley meadows, noted for the excellence of their cheese.

When Wiltshire folk added the metaphor 'and chalk is church, while cheese is chapel', again it was an adequate summing-up of the situation. In most of the villages of the chalk county squire and parson traditionally held sway. The north-west, by contrast, was a country of independent smallholders who were by instinct and upbringing

Puritan and Nonconformist. It is entirely typical that John Maundrell, John Spencer and William Coberley, who were burnt at the stake for heresy in the reign of Queen Mary, were men of Keevil, in the cheese country.

However, there were exceptions to the general division of the county, and Pitton, in the far south-east, was one of them. The reasons are probably neglect by Church authorities and the absence of a resident squire. Even in the Middle Ages, when the village was an annexe of Clarendon Forest, its spiritual welfare was evidently left to the monks of Ivychurch, a good four miles away. The carving-up of the big parish of Alderbury to form three new ones, including the twinned villages of Pitton and Farley, had to wait until late in the nineteenth century, and then the vicar took up residence at Farley. Certainly the village never had a squire on the spot. The door was wide open for nonconformity.

Tradition has it that the Wesleyan denomination arrived at Pitton in the year 1801, when a mason or bricklayer from Andover named Mills moved into the village. The thatched cottage at the end of Slateway in which Jane Mills started a Sunday School and held services was still standing within living memory.

By 1827 a purpose-built chapel had been erected, for a letter written by a visitor to the village in September of that year mentions that on the Sunday evening the whole family went to chapel and heard a good sermon. The land was given by a Whitlock who owned New Manor Farm, Winterslow, a wealthy farmer, and the writer of the letter was a prosperous boatbuilder of Lambeth and a near relation to the Lord Mayor of London, so evidently the Noncomformist movement was not confined to the village artisans and labourers.

St Peter's Church is, of course, very much older. It is probably late twelfth or early thirteenth century and is reputedly older than Salisbury Cathedral. It is a plain cruciform building of flint and stone, largely rebuilt in 1888. Although it sits so low in the ground that the cellar was regularly flooded when 'the springs' rose, it was, before its restoration, even lower. To enter the porch one had to go down a short flight of steps. An unusual feature of the pre-restoration church was a gallery entered by way of a flight of steps *outside* the building. The stumpy steeple is still surmounted by a weathercock fashioned by the village blacksmith, Moses Webb, in the late eighteenth century. In the middle of that century St Peter's had for a time an unusual official in Martha Whitlock, a woman churchwarden.

Throughout the nineteenth century the chapel had the support of a formidable array of members and adherents. After the earliest generation had passed on, their place was taken by a good proportion of the village farmers and by both the local builders, who were doubtless instrumental in the decision to build a new chapel, on a site some distance from the old, in 1888. It is recorded that in 1870 the numbers of scholars on the Sunday School register was eighty-six, which must have included most of the children in the village.

An extract from a diary of a Farley resident reveals that in the last three decades before the First World War that village enjoyed a thriving social calendar, based on the church and also on the fact that Lord Ilchester's agent, Emanuel Parsons, who was the natural leader in all parish affairs, lived there. It was not so at Pitton. Left to its own devices, with little guidance from anyone, Pitton evolved a social life around the chapel. That is not to say that the church lacked its faithful members or was remiss in holding regular Sunday services, but the preponderance of children enrolled in the chapel Sunday School shows where the majority of the villagers felt they 'belonged'.

These were the years of the ascendancy of Nonconformity in national life. Nonconformity was virtually synonymous with the Liberal Party, and this was the era of Gladstone and, later, Lloyd George. It was likewise the era when chapel-going became associated with the temperance movement. To be a member of the chapel you were supposed to be a teetotaller, though only a few decades earlier home-brewed ale rather than tea was served at chapel tea-meetings. Most chapels had, as one of their week-night activities, a Band of Hope, where children were exhorted and even pressurized to sign 'the pledge', vowing total abstinence from alcohol.

Pitton residents who were children in the 1920s and 1930s remember vividly the Thursday evening Band of Hope meetings, one hour long, from seven to eight. Morris Baugh would usually be seen trudging along The Green at about half-past six, his path dimly lit by his horn-sided oil-lantern, on his way to light the chapel oil lamps and to stoke up the 'Tortoise' stove. The children used to love to invite the unwary to 'Put your hand on the tortoise and hear it squeal'! (Alternatively, to spit on the tortoise and watch gobs of spit swirl around until they disappeared.) The meetings were conducted by a rota of the more dedicated chapel members, who were willing to devote an evening a week to a good cause.

The programme followed the typical chapel 'hymn sandwich' – hymn-prayer-hymn-Bible reading-hymn-address-and so on, but the hymns were taken not from the Methodist hymnbook (reserved for Sundays) but from Sankey's and were almost invariably hymns with choruses, such as 'Hold the fort for I am coming', 'Dare to be a Daniel', 'Rescue the perishing'. Sometimes a soloist performed; sometimes someone rendered a recitation (dialect verses were particularly popular), and a good many youngsters had their first nervous experiences of public speaking at Band of Hope. At least once during the autumn/winter schedule a visit from Mr Bill Gambling, of West Grimstead, with his magic lantern, could be expected. It was the nearest most village children ever came to seeing a film.

For the children, however, one of the greatest attractions of Band of Hope was being let out of the house for the evening. 'I'm not going to have you roaming the streets and getting into mischief,' was the attitude of most responsible parents, doubtless recalling what they had got up to when they were young, but one could hardly object to the children's going to Band of Hope. So off they went, with their little flat electric torches in their hands, dutifully to spend an hour singing and fidgeting but afterwards –

heigh-ho! for a glorious game of Fox and Hounds through the black, mysterious countryside! And, as the years passed and maturity loomed, to engage in tentative flirting.

Apart from the use of the Sankey hymnbook, Band of Hope closely resembled Sunday School lessons. For children, and their teachers, Sundays tended to be a bit of a marathon. The morning service at ten-thirty was preceded by Sunday School at nine-thirty. Then a break for Sunday dinner and off to Sunday School again from two to three. Just time to milk the cows, feed the calves, pigs and poultry and partake of Sunday tea, and it was time for the evening service at six. This normally went on until seven-thirty, but the ultra-devout or enthusiastic remained in their pews for an 'after service' or prayer-meeting which often kept going until nine o'clock.

Even those were not the limits. The children of the 1920s were informed that their parents and grandparents used to meet on Sunday mornings at eight, to ask a blessing on the day's services. And as late as the middle 1920s members of Pitton Band would assemble at the corner in the centre of the village at 5.30 p.m. and play rousing hymns until about five to six, when they marched to chaepl for the service. This practice, one feels, owes much to the fact that Ted Whitlock, who was one of the chapel stalwarts, had been since the year 1900 the Pitton bandmaster. He was, however, ably supported by half a dozen or so members of the band, who occupied the choir stalls for the service and accompanied the singing. This was at the time standard practice at village chapels and at a good many village churches. Brass bands were the most popular, but a variety of other instruments, including fiddles, bass viols, clarinets and ophicleides (which the village called 'serpents') also featured. The 'serpents' were usually hand-made and were often so realistic in appearance that one old lady would handle her husband's ophicleide only with a pair of tongs!

The three highspots in the chapel calendar were the Sunday School Anniversary, the Sunday School Outing and the Band of Hope Christmas Tree. Sunday School

Anniversaries were invariably held at Whitsuntide, and Ted Whitlock has left his reminiscences of them when he was a boy. They were very similar a generation later.

Whit Sunday was rather like school Examination Day for us, though perhaps in not quite the same category of horror. Seeing that it was 'Our Day', we were expected to perform and show the adults what we could do. It was expected of us that we would recite verses full of rich Christian sentiment and even that we should sing selected hymns, though the music in general was the province of the choir. Certain music publishers in Yorkshire used to specialize (perhaps they still do) in hymn sheets, with words and tunes especially written for Sunday School anniversaries. As for the verses we were required to learn, they were not called 'poetry' (probably most of them weren't!) nor even 'recitations'; we called them 'anniversary'.

'Now, Ted, have you learnt your anniversary?' Mother would ask.

On the Sunday before Whitsun our mothers and a bevy of old ladies came to Sunday School to hear the final rehearsal. They sat in the back seats, and our Superintendent urged us to shout so that the deaf old soul at the back could hear. Whether we succeeded was more than doubtful, but we could hear them very well. Each recitation was punctuated by interruptions from the rear, ranging from exhortations to speak up to corrections of the subject matter of our verses. After this confusing experience we were subjected to a similar ordeal in the bosom of our families, and throughout the week our mothers wasted precious half-hours in trying to improve our delivery. The result of all this coaching was predictable. On Whit Sunday we tried so hard to remember all we had been told that we forgot our recitations and became entangled in a maze of words.

However, the choir usually made up for our shortcomings. We had a very good choir, with a number of true-toned part-singers. The preachers also were generally chosen for their ability to interest children and to provide plenty of illustrations.

For us children, though, all this was preliminary. Monday was the day to which we all looked forward.

Immediately after dinner we children, together with a large proportion of villagers, flocked to Club Close, behind the chapel, for games and sports. The young men and older boys played cricket; the smaller children were organized by teachers to compete in races or to play 'sheep, sheep, come home' or other time-honoured games. Sometimes there were tugs-of-war and sack races for the bigger children, too. Tea was served on trestle tables erected in the meadow, hot water being carried out from urns in the chapel. Grace was sung. The meal ended, the Superintendent threw handfuls of sweets on the grass for a sweet scramble. The grand finale took the form of a packed rally in the chapel, with a programme which included all the best items from the Sunday services.

Whitsuntide was the recognized season for new clothes. On Sunday morning the little girls, nearly all dressed in white, took their places on the front seats on one side of the chapel, while the boys, uncomfortably clean and ill at ease in their new outfits, occupied the pews on the opposite side of the aisle. Young people had put on their finest apparel, older dames appeared in new bonnets strikingly decorated with feathers, ribbons and wax fruits, fathers and grandfathers sported extravagant buttonholes, and the Sunday School superintendent dodged about in a permanent state of anxiety ...

The Sunday School Outing usually came four or five weeks after the Anniversary, the actual date being dependent on the state of haymaking and harvest. Theoretically there should have been a gap of a couple of weeks between the end of one and the beginning of the other, but the two could overlap, creating difficulties.

Senior citizens still living can just remember when the Sunday School was taken on its annual outing by farm waggons, the destination being the farm of some chapel farmers within ten miles. Pitton children sometimes went to Manor Farm, West Grimstead, where they were able to enjoy sledge rides down the steep, turfy slopes of Whiteparish Hill. Mr Read, the complaisant farmer, provided a pony to haul the sledges back to the top of the hill.

One picture, taken, it is thought, in 1912 or 1913, shows

a Sunday School outing to Amesbury. Between fifty and a hundred people are present, most of whom can still be named.

For outings the village bus was soon superseded by open charabanc, which was pleasant in good weather but presented problems when sudden storms were encountered and the canvas cover had to be erected in haste.

The third of the chapel red-letter days occurred in January, with the Band of Hope Christmas tree. (Curiously the Band of Hope organized a Christmas tree, with tea, presents and an evening service, whereas the Sunday School did not.) Each child received from the tree a little bag of sweets, an orange and a small present. This was the source of most of the electric torches in whose possession small boys delighted. Entertainment at Band of Hope Christmas trees was less restricted than at Sunday School functions. It could even include conjurors or recitations. But Father Christmas was banned, presumably as representing a heathen god.

The children of the 1920s heard recollections of the relationship between church and chapel having been, in times past, something less than harmonious. No doubt in the nineteenth century bigotry existed on both sides. The arguments, it seems, frequently centred around the fact that the village school was Church of England, and the chapel children, or their parents, thought that they were at times discriminated against. Having to learn the catechism was sometimes reckoned a cause for grievance. More than one prejudiced chapel parent had been known to threaten to go to the school and march his or her children out if they were made to recite the catechism.

By the 1920s, however, such disputes were in the receding past, and relations were harmonious – apart, that is, from the church children chanting, as the time drew near,

Rain, rain, go away;
Come on chapel outing day!

to which the chapel kids naturally retaliated.

Towards the end of our period numbers were levelling

out, and the chapel no longer held a numerical preponderance.

To many nineteenth-century villagers the church represented the ancient alliance of squire and parson under which their ancestors had suffered for many a generation. They were instinctive rebels. (It is rightly said that humans naturally vote or demonstrate *against* rather than *for* something. Their instinctive attitude is well represented by Jim Newman, a respected roadman, who, having attended a public meeting and listened to a speaker persuasively arguing for some measure or other, rose up and delivered his memorable opinion: 'I don't understand half what you bin a-talkin' about, Mr Corcorum, but I be *agin* it!')

There was, however, another reason, perhaps even more fundamental. It may sometimes be thought that lack of education is equivalent to a lack of intelligence, but that is not so. The uneducated man may be at a disadvantage because he has fewer facts at his disposal, but he may well have an agile mind well able to make good use of the information he does have. Nowhere has this been more in evidence than in religious affairs. In times when very little literature was available at the peasant level, many villagers knew large sections of the Bible by heart and, with so little else to distract their thoughts as they laboured in the fields, spent much of their time reciting them and thinking about them.

Old William Horner reacted typically when given, by a well-meaning neighbour, an encyclopedia to improve his knowledge. Calling at the cottage days later, he heard cries of 'Praise the Lord!' coming from the old man. Why?

'Well, I read here that the sea in places is seven miles deep, and the Good Book tells me that my sins are taken away and cast into the depths of the sea! Praise the Lord!'

Puritan attitudes were strong and deep-rooted in chapel villages, and one of the basic beliefs was the Protestant tenet of the priesthood of all believers. In other words, a man could come to God direct, without any intermediary; he had no reason to use the offices of priest or parson.

Now that may not be Wesleyan or Methodist doctrine,

but it prevailed in village chapels. Church congregations may have seen their minister only once every three weeks or so, but the chapel people were visited by theirs, in general, no more than once a quarter. Even then, to them he was a 'townee'. They listened politely (or sometimes protestingly) to what he had to say and carried on in their old ways. Sermons were preached from their pulpits twice or more on Sunday, but the preachers were local preachers, often villagers like themselves.

That the village chapel set-up was a model of democracy could hardly be denied. At the beginning of our period the leader was John Webb, the village roadman. His predecessor in office was Helen Fry, a widow who, having lost one husband in an accident which left her with ten children to support, not many years later married another, also an agricultural labourer. The new partnership soon produced four more children, but Helen coped efficiently with the responsibility, besides starting a women's meeting (social and educational as well as religious) and eventually taking over the chapel leadership. John Webb's successor was Ted Whitlock, a former pauper lad who had attained the status of farmer (such as it amounted to, in Pitton!), but he was no more than first among equals, among whom were Morris Baugh, the thatcher, Will Sheppard, a carter, and Will Clark. Early in the 1920s Owen Griffin, settling in Parsonage Farm, automatically became associated with the leadership, as did Stanley Horner, who in the 1920s had the new village shop built.

Apart from a visit from a Salisbury minister about once a quarter, the Sunday service (and week-night meetings) were conducted by local preachers – as, indeed, the services in most village chapels still are. Their calibre varied, some being exceptionally able and some mediocre. An outstanding preacher, still remembered, was 'Shepherd' Keel, who kept sheep on Salisbury Plain not far from Stonehenge. William Herrington, a smallholder, was a born orator who could speedily attract a crowd in an open-air meeting on a market day. Arthur Horner, who suffered from a slight speech impediment and was often carried away by his emotional oratory, had a remarkable dramatic gift. His sermon on Jeremiah in the miry pit is still remembered:

'This morning, my friends, we find poor old Jeremiah stuck in the mud at the bottom of a miry pit, but never fear, my friends, we shall get en out avore dinner-time!'

And when the sermon reached its dramatic climax, the old chap was reaching over the side of the pulpit, pulling so hard on an imaginary rope that his collar stud came unfastened, the collar retreated to the back of his neck, and tears mingled with the sweat streaming down his furrowed cheeks.

'Here he comes, my friends! Pull hard! Pull hard! One more heave an' we shall have en out!'

It was Arthur Horner who painted a graphic picture of Jacob leaving home, his mother 'standing at the door of the little whitewashed cottage, crying and waving her handkerchief'. And another of the domestic life of Jesse and his sons:

'Old Jesse had seven sons. All boys! That were a handful for any man. But what it would have bin like if they'd bin all girls hardly bears thinkin' about.'

And he went on to envisage Mrs Jesse's wash-day with seven little shirts hanging on the clothes line ...

Attendances at Sunday services were excellent, by our later standards. Each family of chapel-goers had its recognized pew, though pew rent, mentioned back in 1837, had been abolished. The back two seats were not reserved for anyone in particular but were regarded as the province of the village lads and unmarried men. In winter they were generally occupied, for what else was there to do in Pitton on a dark Sunday evening? Even Salisbury, six miles away, could offer few other attractions, before the age of cinemas. However, a preacher like Arthur Horner had good entertainment value, and there was always a chance for the young of pairing-off with a girl after the service.

Every few years the chapel staged a series of revival meetings, conducted by professional evangelists. A 'campaign' would normally last ten days or a fortnight and consisted of 'hot gospel' meetings and/or prayer meetings every night of the week, working up to a climax on the last evening, when the evangelist went all out for conversions. The atmosphere must have been very similar to that of fundamentalist gospel meetings in the western and southern states of America, and was so supercharged with emotion that inevitably the evangelist secured numbers of converts. Within a year or so many of them had to be written off as backsliders. Some, however, became genuinely 'born-again' Christians and remained loyal all their lives.

The shadow of ancient wrongs by squire and parson and a consequent latent anti-clericalism lingered over late-Victorian village life and even survived into the inter-war-years. Many chapel-goers were suspicious of even their own ministers. Considerable numbers of those who were regular in their attendance at services refused to become members because that, it seemed to them, involved taking Holy Communion from the hands of the minister (alias the priest), which offended their deepest principles. They reconciled their attitude with Christ's injunction regarding the breaking of bread and drinking of wine by the interpretation that what Christ meant was that His disciples should remember Him at every meal they ate. For that reason, grace before meat was a widely observed custom, taken very seriously.

Someone walking in the woods once chanced on Alfred Annetts, a Winterslow woodman, as he was about to begin his mid-day meal. In the yard outside his little hurdle hut he was sitting on a rough bench at a rustic table. On a spotless white cloth were places laid for two – two knives, two tumblers, two hunks of bread and cheese and pickles.

'Expecting a visitor, then, Alfred?'

Came the reply, 'I always do this. If my Master should suddenly appear one day, I wouldn't want Him to think He was unexpected.'

Nor were the chapel congregation appreciative of learned expository sermons.

'That was a fine sermon!' a village critic told his minister. 'A fine sermon – to judge by the quantity of

Threshing in the Thirties

Pitton's first tractor—note the iron strakes—hitched to a horse-type seed drill

Threshing with an old-type steam engine

The Pitton Sheep Shearing Gang about 1880

Isaac Dear surrounded by sheep cribs and stools in the interior of the workshop at Winterslow

Rick making, *c.*1939. The elevator was an innovation

Ted Mills, tractor-driver

Charlie Whitlock claiming to be a poacher!

Cutting grass for hay

paper! We had enough paper to set fire to Salisbury Cathedral. But if we'd had a bit less paper and a bit more fire, it'd have been better for everybody!'

Understandably, the Salvation Army made a strong appeal. The story of how the first Salvation Army band came into existence is well documented. Hearing that the Army was to hold a service in Salisbury market-place one Sunday evening, when William Booth's work was in its infancy, Charles Fry, a regular worshipper in Alderbury chapel though with close links with Pitton, decided to discover what it was all about. Being a member of the village band, he took his cornet with him, as he always did to a service. And when the singing started, he accompanied it on the cornet. Always quick to recognize a good idea, William Booth seized on this one, and before long bands were an integral part of Salvation Army life.

In Pitton in the 1920s and 1930s the Army publications, *The War Cry* and *The Young Soldier*, had a much bigger circulation than *The Methodist Recorder* and the *The Church Times*.

Three of Arthur Whitlock's four daughters became Salvation Army officers. Most outstanding of the Army personalities to originate from Pitton, however, was William Baugh, who, starting life as a village ploughboy of the same generation as Arthur Whitlock, became a convert and joined the Army as an officer. Rising to the rank of brigadier, he was one of the pioneers entrusted with the establishment of the Army's work in America. Speaking, in his old age, at Sunday School Anniversary services, he used to like to relate how, conducting a campaign in the backwoods of Maine, he met a woman with whom he found he had much in common. Both of them had been converted in Pitton chapel.

He sometimes brought with him a great carriage umbrella about which he told tales of the early days of the Army in Whitechapel. When gangs of thugs tried to break up the meetings, he used to lay about him with the umbrella. A big, muscular man, not unlike Ian Paisley in looks, he was also possessed of a powerful voice and an emphatic manner of speaking. He provided effective protection for the Salvation Army lasses.

It was a pity that some acrimony at times invaded the relationship between church and chapel in Victorian times and found expression in the school curriculum, for Pitton had an excellent village school, founded in 1853. It was, however, a Church of England school, and the more bigoted chapel folk regarded it with suspicion. They did not appreciate that they should have been glad that the youngsters were getting any religious instruction at all.

However, objections or no objections, all the Pitton children in the second half of the nineteenth century and the first four decades of the twentieth duly attended Pitton school and emerged with a good, solid, basic education. In the early days fees of a few pence a week were payable. Ted Whitlock recalled that, as a pauper boy, his penny was paid by the Relieving Officer, but that arrangement had been abandoned before living memory begins. There are traditions that prior to 1853 dames' schools existed, held by indigent widows in their cottages, but little is known about them.

It was remembered that in the 1880s a schoolmaster, a Mr Taylor, had once presided over Pitton school, but that was exceptional. Normally the head teacher was a schoolmistress and, although again there were exceptions, she was generally either an elderly lady filling in time before retirement or a girl just out of college. The situation improved in the late 1920s and 1930s. The infant teacher was usually unqualified but the generation of children in the 1920s remember with pleasure and gratitude the kind middle-aged Miss Packer who gave them their introduction to school life.

The school building, single-storeyed, was divided by folding doors into two unequal compartments, the Big Room and the Little Room. The child graduated from the Little Room to the Big Room at the age of seven or eight, so the Big Room teacher had to cope with all ages from seven to fourteen (school-leaving age). Despite that, the supreme advantage possessed by village schoolchildren was individual attention. Although the head teacher in the

Big Room might be confronted each morning by fifty children, she was able to split them up into manageable sections and, if a reasonable disciplinarian, could concentrate on one group at a time while the others were busy at written exercises.

She dealt with essentials – namely, 'reading, writing and arithmetic'. History, geography and art were occasional extras, and religious instruction was, of course, not neglected, but children of the 1920s can remember only one Big Room teacher who tried to interest them in nature study. Miss Packer showed a little more versatility. Children of that period recall her teaching them how to make cowslip-balls by tying together the heads of cowslips picked in the meadows!

Victorian children had to write on slates, wiped clean at the end of each exercise by a rag, a handkerchief or a sleeve. By the 1920s the school was affluent enough to provide exercise books for all but the primary class. That was one of the few amenities, for, like every other building in the village, the school lacked piped water and sanitation. The school building, imaginatively and efficiently planned, had a small but adequate porch equipped with coat-pegs and wash-basins, but no water ever dampened the wash-basins. The children had only a vague idea what they were for. Around the back the lavatories were perched on a bank overhanging the yard of Parsonage Farm. On Saturdays one of Owen Griffin's men had the task of removing the buckets and emptying them on the dung-heap.

The school playground for the Big Room was fairly minute, – about five yards square. It served for nothing but assembly before school and for the mid-morning break. School was for work, not for playing games and taking exercise. School was listening to teachers, writing in exercise books, reading textbooks and taking down simple sums from the blackboard. School was always, invariably, indoors.

Outside, however, the children had ample opportunity for exercise. The meadows, fields and woods were their natural domain. The life of the village enveloped them.

Most of the parents worked on farms, and there was always something to do on farms, or in a family garden or allotment. It was an exceptional boy (girls were seldom as lucky) who had no animals (farm livestock or pets) to feed, water and litter up before and after school. June and July saw all hands, including small ones, busy in the hayfields till after dark. The long school holiday that coincided with the corn harvest was originally planned not as a break for a seaside holiday but simply as a recognition of the fact that no power on earth would get children into school when harvest beckoned.

The children of the 1920s were told that in their parents' day the school target was the fourth standard. When a child reached that level, he or she was entitled to leave school. As a natural result the only reward for the gifted child was a curtailment of school life. At the end of the nineteenth century the required standard was attained at the age of twelve. By the 1920s the demarcation line of the fourth standard seems to have been abandoned in favour of a statutory school-leaving age of fourteen. For all generations from the mid-nineteenth century onwards, however, no children, except those mentally unable to learn, left school without being able to read, write and do basic arithmetic.

Few village children ever had the benefit of higher education. Apart from a few private schools in Salisbury, the only one with a claim to be a public or secondary school was Bishop Wordsworth's School. In the late 1920s a regular bus service and a proliferation of private cars opened the door to increased educational possibilities, but before that only three Pitton boys are known to have received a secondary education. One was Willoughby Talbot, the keeper's son, who later became a schoolmaster; another was Eric Bell, gifted with considerable artistic talent; the third was Ralph Whitlock, author of this book.

In theory, free secondary education was available to village children, both boys and girls, who passed a scholarship examination at the age of eleven. In practice very few Pitton children ever took the examination. In the crucial year for Ralph Whitlock, the position of head teacher at Pitton was occupied by a succession of temporary schoolmistresses, mostly girls fresh from college, and the time for examinations slipped by unnoticed. With Ralph's twelfth birthday looming in Febuary 1926, his father, Ted, went in the autumn of 1925 to see Reuben Bracher, the formidable headmaster of Bishop Wordsworth's School, to enquire whether the boy could be admitted. Yes, he could. The headmaster was empowered to take a certain number of fee-paying pupils, for the princely sum of two guineas a term.

Ted had assumed that the school year naturally coincided with the calendar year and was surprised to learn that Ralph had already missed a term in the current year. So a new bike, school uniform and satchel were hurriedly purchased and Ralph began his secondary education in January 1926. He was decanted into the lowest form of all – a kindergarten.

At that time Bishop Wordsworth's School still catered for girls as well as boys. South Wilts Grammar School for girls was opened about two years later.

In retrospect it seems a tough decision to require an eleven-year-old boy to cycle six hilly miles to school and six back again in dead of winter. Even the main road was rough-surfaced and rutty, and the return journey had sometimes to be made after dark (the bicycle lamp was acetylene). But no one thought the arrangement in any respect unusual, and Ralph accepted it as natural. In summer he often shortened the journey by two miles by taking footpaths through the woods – a lovely ride beneath a dappled tree canopy, though with several very steep hills and too muddy to be practicable in rain weather.

He enjoyed the school life at Bishop Wordworth's School, made many friends and did reasonably well academically. At first, however, he found he had a lot of leeway to make up, through deficiencies in his education at Pitton school. For instance, when, after his first two terms, he found himself moved into a form which took Latin and French, he remembers being considerably handicapped by his ignorance of English grammar. His

10   *The Daily Round*

Had it not been for Sundays, the days and weeks would have merged into each other with little to mark their passing. If nothing else, Sundays were different. Otherwise life unrolled itself according to a familiar and almost immutable pattern. A diarist might well have found himself reduced to the level of 'Got up; had breakfast; went to work; had supper; went to bed.'

Early rising was the norm. On the farms, where most of the villagers worked, the hours were from seven to five, with overtime when necessary. For carters and men working with horses, the day started rather earlier, for they were expected to be at the stable in time to give the animals their breakfast, clean out and renew the litter, harness the horses, lead them out into the yard for water and have them ready to start work by half-past seven.

At the other end of the day, the carters were allowed to knock off work in time to do all those chores and have the horses back in the stable by five o'clock. However, they were then required to pay an evening visit to the stable to see that the horses were comfortable and to give them another meal to see them through the night. The standard conclusion to any winter evening entertainment in the village hall by a dialect comedian was, 'Ah well, I must bid ee good-night now. I got to go and rack up the 'osses!'

In summer the horses were often put out to grass overnight and, if they were young and lively, the horseman sometimes had an energetic half hour catching them in the mornings.

The process by which cows replaced sheep on the farms was a gradual one – first a single cow, then, after a year or so, another one or two. The maximum number in a Pitton herd in the 1920s and 1930s was about a dozen. So, to start with, milking the cow or cows was just another chore to be undertaken before breakfast, like feeding the pigs and poultry and attending to the horses. When the herd had grown to eight or ten, the task was becoming somewhat more formidable. Nevertheless, attempts were made to stick to the old routine.

A celebrated story that went the rounds in farming circles in the 1930s concerned an Oxfordshire farmer from the top shelf, with hundreds of acres and a full complement of employees, including an annual batch of farm pupils. When the pupils arrived, they were told that their working day began at half-past-seven, for which they were prepared. Apparently as an afterthought he informed them that, of course, they were expected to attend to all the chores, such as feeding the animals and cleaning out their stalls, and also the milking. To their consternation, they found there were 120 cows!

The superseding of sheep by cows was such a gradual process that it involved virtually no changes in technique. The recognized method of milking a cow was to sit on a three-legged stool, dig your head into her side and milk with a tilted bucket. Most milkers spurted the first drops of milk onto their hands, to make them soft and supple. The increase in numbers of cows involved no change in technique. It was simply a matter of employing more milkers or of taking a bit longer over the job if the farmer did it himself.

Even before the era of milk production for profit, most farmers (and some cottagers) kept a house cow, and a few of them made butter. The milk was left to stand in shallow pans until the cream could be skimmed off with a skimmer. Once a week the butter was made in a rotary churn, and a little surplus butter was sometimes sold in the village. (Milk had always been supplied to neighbours who did not keep cows and who brought their milk-cans to the door.) As the herds multiplied, however, farmers had to consider the commercial possibilities. In the 1920s Lionel White started a milk-collection service, taking churns daily to United Dairies in Salisbury. One or two farmers, though, including Ted Whitlock, expanded a butter-making business, purchasing one of the new-fangled separators and appropriate butter-making accessories. The butter was sold, in half-pound pats, at 2s 4d per pound to customers in Salisbury.

There was in Pitton no tradition of cheese-making. A very cheap cheese could be purchased from Aunt Polly's shop and was extensively used, but its hardness and dryness were a byword. A popular yarn of the time concerned a gipsy woman who called at one of the farms, selling pegs, and, having received a friendly reception, tried pushing her luck.

'You don't happ'n to have a bit of cheese to spare?' she asked, and spun a tale about having only dry bread to eat.

The good wife brought her a wedge of the familiar mouse-trap cheese. After eyeing it with apprehension and testing it with her thumb, the gipsy enquired,

'Do you happen to have trouble with your eyes, Missus?'

'Why, yes, I must say they are failing a bit.'

'Well, medear, you hold that cheese over a fire, and

catch the first drop of fat that falls from it and rub it on your eyes. That'll cure 'em! It'd cure anything!'

Most of the old West Country cheeses tended to be hard and dry. A good deal of time and energy have been spent in recent years researching the celebrated Dorset Blue Vinny cheese, reputed to have been extinct for several decades. Ultimately certain cheese-makers attempted to revive the old tradition, introducing a delicious blue-veined cheese which they called Dorset Blue. But it wasn't Dorset Blue Vinny. That was a hard, cottager's cheese made from skimmed milk, whereas this was a splendid gourmet cheese. And the likeliest reason why Blue Vinny became extinct was that the methods used in making it were too unhygienic!

The attitude of old-time countrymen towards hygiene is illustrated by a tale of a Wiltshire farmer (not a Pitton one, it is to be hoped) who, soon after the Milk Marketing Board was established in 1933, was surprised one morning by the early arrival of a Board inspector.

'You be come avore I be ready for thee,' he complained. 'Never mind. Shan't keep ee long. Just wait while I strains this yer milk.'

With that he undid his belt, whipped out the front of his shirt, tightened it over the mouth of the churn and strained the milk through it!

He was most indignant at losing his licence. Couldn't understand it!

The farmer, of course, helped any employees with all the morning tasks; that was the natural order of things. When all the chores were finished, however, and field work was in progress, he could go indoors for a leisurely breakfast. In Ted Whitlock's household the breakfast hour was from approximately half past seven to half past eight. It included a Bible reading and a short extempore prayer. Pitton had no telephones in those days, but if there had been any they would almost certainly have been taken off the hook to avoid interruption at breakfast time.

The system whereby unmarried farmworkers lived in the farmhouse and ate at the farmer's table in lieu of part of their wages had largely died out by the twentieth century, though Ted Whitlock usually had one or more lads sharing the life of the family. At Bower's Farm, the home of the Seawards, provision had been made in the architecture for the accommodation of unmarried staff. A rough ladder and steps over the chimney corner and bread-oven led to the unceilinged attics where the boys slept. This had not been used for the purpose, however, within living memory.

After breakfast the cows were taken out to pasture, except in hard weather in winter. It tended to be a time-consuming task, especially for those farmers with no home paddocks. The time saved in winter by the cows staying in the yard was occupied by the preparations of their rations. That involved carting, cleaning and slicing large quantities of mangolds and swedes, the slicing machine being operated manually. Cattlecake, too, was usually bought in big slabs, like tombstones, and had to be broken up in a cake-crusher. Later, when petrol engines became available, some farmers installed mills for grinding their own corn for feeding livestock, but that was not until the late 1930s.

Most of the farmers kept poultry, in a manner which would be highly approved today, for it was entirely free-range. The usual accommodation for the hens consisted of portable houses, on small iron wheels, each holding about thirty. In spring and summer these houses were parked in some convenient pasture. As soon as a cornfield was harvested, the houses were moved to the stubble, and the hens found their own living on shed grains for the next six weeks or so, moving around the farm as the food supply on each field became exhausted. In winter the houses came to rest in a rickyard or farmyard, though some farmers turned a compartment of a barn into a deep-litter house.

Although taking the fowls 'out stubbling' struck the farmers as being an economical procedure, relieving them of the necessity of feeding the birds at a season when they were moulting anyway, it was, in fact, quite labour-intensive – though that hardly mattered with wages at thirty shillings a week. Many of the cornfields were situated a mile or so from home, so every other day a horse-drawn water-barrel had to spend an hour or two replenishing their water supply. This was generally an early morning job, so that the man could let the fowls out at the same time, but someone had to do the rounds again in the late evening, to shut the fowls in again. This was an absolutely essential task, whose neglect could result in massacre by foxes. And it could never be hurried, for the hens refused to go to bed till well after sunset; nor could they be chased to roost. So in the long days of summer 'shutting up the fowls' provided an evening chore, often unwelcome, after ten o'clock at night.

Hatching the next generation of chicks occupied farmers' wives for several months from late February onwards. The natural method was used exclusively; nobody in the village possessed an incubator. Broody hens were incarcerated in coops, orange boxes and apple barrels to sit on clutches of thirteen eggs each – always thirteen: it was considered unlucky to sit a hen on an even number of eggs. To be allowed to ease one's hand under a gently clucking hen and feel against her warm flesh the little balls of fluff which were her newly hatched chicks was a lovely experience sampled by most village children in those days.

For the first week or so the chicks were fed on chopped, hardboiled eggs and breadcrumbs, after which they were gradually weaned to proprietary chick-crumbs and grains of wheat. No attempt was made to distinguish between the sexes. Sex-linking was unknown and, anyway, most of the poultry were complete mongrels. So cockerels and pullets ran together until they began to take a sexual interest in each other. Generally the cockerels remained as scavengers in and around the farmyard while the hens and pullets were stubbling, and batches were often confined in pens for the Christmas market.

Farm-produced cockerels, generally at least six pounds in weight and often heavier, were a luxury product. As such, they were for sale, not for home consumption. You could get two joints of meat for the price of one good cockerel. The poultry eaten at the farmer's table consisted of old boiling fowls, whose egg-laying days were over.

Some farms kept ducks, and both Owen Griffin and Ted Whitlock had flocks of turkeys for Christmas consumption. Both ducks and turkeys came to the farm in the form of eggs which were hatched by hens. Disease was often rife and mortality heavy among the turkeys. It was not appreciated that the hens were often the carriers of disease which affected them only mildly but were lethal for young turkeys. When, eventually, this fact was realized and day-old turkey poults, hatched by incubator, were kept in strict isolation from the moment they arrived at the farm, much better results were achieved.

A few geese were kept – Owen Griffin usually had a breeding nucleus on his pond – but they were not popular. They laid only limited numbers of eggs, were difficult to kill and even more difficult to pluck, and the ganders were bullies. Nevertheless, the real reason for their scarcity was perhaps credence given to the old saying that, 'Where geese are kept, the farmer's wife wears the breeches'! In times past, geese evidently were one of the perks of the farmer's wife, providing her with pin-money, but they made such a foul mess of the home pasture that no self-respecting farmer would have them on the place, unless compelled by his wife!

Of other livestock, tame rabbits were kept by many schoolboys, for whom they were useful objects for barter. There are memories of the raucous calls of guinea-fowl echoing across the valley, and farmers who brought home from market allegedly bargain lots of muscovy ducks soon wished they hadn't, for the drakes proved worse bullies than ganders. The only apiary in the village was kept by Willoughby Talbot, who, although sometimes stung by the bees, seemed to regard their stings with indifference. Children marvelled to see him, innocent of net veil, nonchalantly pick stinging bees from his cheeks and eyelids.

The shepherd tended to live apart from village life, his flock living, as a rule, in the more distant fields. In summer the sheep were, of course, on the downs, and in the lambing season confined in lambing pens, but for the rest of the time they lived mostly in the arable fields. The shepherd's daily task then was to pitch a new hurdle pen for his flock every day, thus rationing out the turnips, vetches, clover or other crops that had been grown especially for them. The water barrel was, however, kept busy supplying the sheep with drinking water, and in winter carting hay for the flock was similarly a priority.

As all the Pitton farmers, with the exception of Owen Griffin, were of local peasant stock, their thinking was naturally dominated by tradition, and nowhere more so than in their attitude towards pigs. Pigs were the peasant's, the cottager's, livestock. A pig was an adjunct of every thrifty household. It lived in a sty at the bottom end of the garden, next to the privy and the rhubarb patch, the rhubarb thriving naturally by its proximity to both. The sty was a small but compact edifice of board slabs, roofed with corrugated iron, though not so long ago with thatch. It had three compartments – namely, an outside pen, interior sleeping quarters and a passage wide enough to hold a stool on which was perched a mixing tub and a bag of barley meal. When the church was renovated in 1888, many of the old tombstones found their way into the sexton's pigsty.

Feeding the pig was a regular morning and evening chore; the pig soon issued its own reminder if neglected. Most cottagers found time to attend to it before and after work, but the task was one which most wives readily undertook if necessary. All household scraps went into the pig bucket. Irreverently, children chanted,

> Dearly beloved brethren, don't you think it a sin.
>> When you peel potatoes, to throw away the skin?
>> The skin feeds the pig, the pig feeds you.
>> Dearly beloved brethren, is not this true?

In many households the pig developed into a sort of household pet, to be given available titbits. Cottager's disinclined for worship on Sunday mornings spent many a restful hour down the garden, communing with the pig, safely out of the way of a wife busy preparing dinner.

Its favoured status did not, however, save the pig from

the fate of all pigs in late autumn. On a frosty morning in November or early December it was led forth, protesting, to the pig-killing stool, where its throat was cut. Ted Whitlock, in addition to his many other roles, was regarded as the village pig-killing expert. In the late 1920s the presence of a licensed butcher with a 'humane killer' was legally required, and Wesley Horner, the Winterslow butcher, used to come over to Pitton for the purpose, but not much earlier the pig-killer got busy with a butcher's knife without the formality of a preliminary stunning.

Pig-killing followed a well-marked ritual. Once the pig had lost consciousness, its throat was cut deeply, and the spurting blood was caught in a basin for making black pudding. Lizzie Collins was the recognized expert in the practice of this culinary art and was a regular attendant at pig-killings.

The pig then had to be singed and scrubbed – or 'swaled', to use the technical term. An expert pig-killer would so arrange his operation that the pig collapsed on a prepared bed of dry straw, which was quickly set on fire. Men made torches of the straw to burn off the bristles which the flames could not reach. As the fire died, the carcase was 'flowsed down' with buckets of water, during which process the men scraped furiously at the bristles. Some used knives, but convention said that the proper tool was the edge of a pewter candlestick.

The carcase was then manhandled onto a wheelbarrow and conveyed to the gibbet designed for it. Farmers used the great beams of their barns, but cottagers often had a timber frame erected or the purpose. The weight of the pig was taken by a gamril (a kind of wooden yoke) inserted behind the sinews of its hind legs, and the carcase was hoisted aloft by main force. The pig-killer then stationed himself against the pig's belly, with his apron stretched tight around the carcase. With a sharp knife he made a cut from end to end and proceeded to extract the intestines, which tumbled into his apron. Men on either side helped to support their weight. The pig-killer needed to know just where to make his key cuts and how to avoid puncturing unsavoury organs, such as the gall-bladder.

The carcase was then left to cool overnight, with a cloth wrapped around its snout to protect it from roving cats. The offal, which by now had been transferred to a galvanized bath, was taken into the kitchen for sorting and processing. Almost every cottage housewife was adept at this operation. Chitterlings were detached and cleansed; liver, lights, kidneys, heart and melts were separated and set aside; the bladder was set aside for a child's football. Certain delicacies were best used for faggots, others for brawn; fat was melted down for lard, and the skimmings made delicious 'scraps' or 'scratchen'. For a week or two after pig-killing the household enjoyed a gourmet cuisine without stint.

As most of the villagers were related in some way, there was much exchanging of titbits, as one pig-killing followed another, the season of feasting often lasting nearly to Christmas. Even the poorest families fared well at this season, when abundance made householders generous.

Meantime arrangements were being made for future supplies. Hams were pickled or smoked and roasted. Sides of bacon were thoroughly salted in wooden silts and then eventually suspended on bacon racks under the kitchen ceiling. Eyepieces were similarly preserved or were dismembered to make Bath chaps, the odd scraps of meat being valued ingredients for brawn. The brains were regarded as a particular delicacy. Prudent housewives could thus ensure a supply of meat for the greater part of the year.

Such was the status of the cottage pig in the life of the village that politicians who were aware of its importance did their best to foster it. Cottagers were encouraged to form Pig Clubs, and one was formed at Pitton. Pig-owners paid sixpence per pig and were entitled to its value, or to what happened to be in the kitty, if a pig fell sick and died. Piglets were inspected on arrival, again by Ted Whitlock, who was secretary of the Pig Club, to make sure they were healthy, and it was he who had to be informed of a death and to meet the subsequent demand for payment.

As many of the farmers had graduated to their present

status from humbler beginnings, they tended to stick to the pig-keeping methods they knew. There was no specialist pig-keeping. It was simply a matter of keeping eight or ten pigs instead of one, but in the same sort of sty and on the same diet. No farmer kept a breeding herd. The store pigs were bought in Salisbury market and the fat pigs sold there. The farmers, however, mostly opted to join the Pig Club, which eventually foundered because it was not intended to deal with commercial enterprises and had insufficient funds to meet a demand for compensation for several casualties at once.

While autumnal pig-killing heralded a season of unaccustomed luxury in the matter of food, for the rest of the year meals were much plainer, even frugal. Most families had a roast for Sunday dinner (mid-day), though in cottages the meat was often boiled bacon, or perhaps rabbit – there were always plenty of rabbits to be had, in those pre-myxomatosis days.

> Rabbits hot and rabbits cold,
> Rabbits young and rabbits old,
> Rabbits tender, rabbits tough.
> Thank the Lord, I've had enough.

was a grace that youngsters used to chant when they thought their elders weren't listening. It is remembered, though, that, in one hard-pressed household of parents and thirteen children, on Sundays the mother used to serve the pudding before the meat course, in the hope that by the time the meat was on their plates the youngsters would have had the edge taken off their appetites.

Enquiries among surviving children of the 1920s have revealed nothing startling about the menus for breakfast and other meals. Oatmeal porridge was the only breakfast cereal known, this being before the cornflakes era. Several persons have said they had only bread-and-butter and jam for breakfast, though others enjoyed a hearty breakfast of eggs, bacon and fried bread. Quite a common dish was tea-kettle broth, which consisted of lumps of bread dropped in a basin of hot water, with a pat or two or butter and a sprinkling of pepper and salt added. Bread and pork dripping was very appetizing, mutton dripping not so attractive.

The author remembers sitting on his father's lap when he came home from market and being fed on mashed potatoes, with salt and pepper, spread on bread-and-butter, which he regarded as a delicacy. Others recall seeing their fathers, on returning from work, enjoying a meal of cheese on toast, served on an enamel plate. For days on end, though, breakfast, dinner and supper all consisted of cold bacon, mostly fat.

Eggs were not on the menu as often as might be expected, for they were saleable. Poultry featured in the diet only when a very old hen, whose laying days were over, was boiled. The era of the stockpot was only just over the horizon – indeed, hardly that in some households. Ted Whitlock had been told that the kitchen range that now occupied the chimney corner of his house was the first ever to be installed in Pitton. Before that, cooking was done in the stockpot hanging over the open fire on the hearth. In general the pot was kept a-simmering all day and every day, new ingredients being added as they became available. Virtually everything edible went into the stockpot, the vegetables (and particularly potatoes) being kept separate by means of home-made nets, which could be fished out at will. Dumplings were added from time to time. When an adequate crust formed over the stock, it was skimmed off and used as a covering for puddings, sweet as often as savoury. A mixture of sweet and savoury was merely irrelevant – it was all food.

A dish popular in those times though hardly ever featured in modern cookbooks were lambs-tail pies or puddings. For hygienic reasons lambs had their tails docked a few days after birth, and the tails were regarded as a culinary delicacy – a spring-time treat much as peewit eggs and nettle-top soup.

Bread was still being made in many village ovens in the 1920s. The method was standard. An entire brushwood faggot was pushed into the oven and allowed to burn to ashes. When the iron door was opened and the ashes were raked out, if a special 'fire brick' at the far end of the coffin-shaped orifice glowed red-hot, the oven was ready. If not, more fuel was added. Most housewives used home-produced flour, from Pitton wheat ground by the Winterbourne miller. Widows, paupers and the wives of some farm labourers used to go gleaning, gathering up the stray ears of corn from the harvest field, most of them managing to salvage a sack or two of grain, which was sufficient for a good many loaves of bread, and it was excellent bread, too – in the form of cottage loaves. When, in later years, the big firms which had come to monopolize the bread-making industry declared that they must have a high proportion of hard Canadian or American wheat because the soft English varieties did not produce good bread, the village folk frankly did not believe them. They knew otherwise.

Most housewives baked cakes. The author remembers his mother, who tended to put things off till the last moment, often saying on Saturday evening, 'Oh well, I must rub up some cake for tea tomorrow.' Those cakes usually took the form of shapeless 'rock cakes', with dried fruit and orange peel, which were excellent when new but inclined to become rock-like if kept for a few days (not that they often were!). Seed cakes and dough cakes were popular. Concerning the latter, menfolk used to joke about 'Twelve Apostle Cake' – eleven apostles fetched the dough, sugar and water, while the twelfth, Judas, ran away with the currants! Powder cakes were made according to much the same recipe as rock cakes, but sponge cakes were almost unknown.

Wiltshire's speciality cake is, of course, a rolled-in lardy cake, and a good many experts in the art were to be found in Pitton kitchens. It was particularly favoured in the weeks after pig-killing, when lard was plentiful. A recipe is appended below.

Wiltshire Lardy Cake

1 lb flour	½ pint warm milk and water
2 teaspoons salt	½ lard
1 tablespoon sugar	½ sugar
¼ oz yeast	6 oz sultanas

Mix salt and flour. Add warm liquid to sugar and yeast. Leave for a while to rise. Pour into flour and mix well. Cover and leave in warm place to rise until it has doubled in size or is level with the top of the bowl. The warmer the kitchen, the quicker the dough will rise.

When the dough has risen roll and shape it. Spread over it half the lard, sugar and sultanas. Fold and roll out again. Spread over it the rest of the lard, fruit and sugar. Fold over and roll out again. Fit into a greased and sugared tin. Leave to rise for 20 minutes. Bake for 40-45 minutes.

This makes a cake of roasting-tin size. For a smaller cake, use half the ingredients.

Except for special reasons, such as Christmastime and harvest, the housewife's week ran to an almost immutable routine. When a village girl married, she knew just what her tasks would be on each day of the week for the rest of her life. Monday was wash day, Tuesday was ironing day. Wednesday was bedroom day. Thursday was cooking day. Friday was cleaning and polishing day, Saturday was the preparations for the Sabbath. Only a crisis, such as the arrival of a baby, permitted any relaxation of the rules. Even then, whoever looked after the wife while she was in bed followed the familiar routine.

Preparations for the Sabbath included drawing sufficient water from the well for the Monday wash. It was stored in large earthenware pans with wooden lids. The housewife would get up before daybreak on Mondays to get the copper boiling. The copper usually was made of copper and was an integral part of the house, set in concrete next to the bread-oven.

While the copper was warming up, the dirty clothes, which had been put to soak in a tub of cold water over the week-end, were taken out and put through the mangle. The housewife also prepared the starch – two tablespoon-fuls stirred in a bowl, and the blue. When hot water was available in the copper, it was dipped out into a tub, fortified with soap, and had the dirty clothes immersed in it for a good scrubbing. The soap was bar soap, from Aunt Polly's shop – no soap powders or detergents in those days – and the scrubbing was made more effective by the use of a corrugated wooden scrubbing-board. Then through the mangle once more, until finally, when the clothes were white as new, they went into the copper for a boiling.

Even then, the process was not finished. In due course the clothes were hoisted out of the copper, with the aid of a copper-stick, and dumped in a tub for rinsing. After two lots of rinsing, in blue water, they were put through the mangle once again and then, at last, hung on the clothes line to dry.

Says an informant who remembers wash day in her mother's farm kitchen when she was a girl,

'Mind you, when the clothes were on the line we hadn't finished. There were all the outdoor clothes to wash, like grandad's smock, and all the farm sacks. Sacks were used time and again, until they were worn in holes, and then they were usually patched till they were threadbare. And when sulphate of ammonia was introduced and we had to scrub the manure sacks, that was a hellish job. Tatie sacks were a trial, too. We used the water from the general wash for doing the sacks, and by the time we'd washed a dozen or two tatie sacks the water was half mud. But it was just as good, if not better, for watering the garden when everything was finished.' And she repeated the old wash-day rhyme:

They that wash on Monday have all the week to dry.
They that wash on Tuesday do not go far awry.
They that wash on Wednesday are not too much to blame.
They that wash on Thursday wash for shame.
They that wash on Friday wash in need.
They that wash on Saturday are dirty sluts indeed!

Of course, washing on Sunday would have been so unthinkable that there was no line in the verse to describe such infamy.

In the era of the carrier's cart, mothers of families would usually go to Salisbury on shopping expeditions twice a year. One was at Easter or between Easter and Whitsuntide, the other in October, to coincide with Salisbury Fair. New bonnets or spring outfits normally made their first appearance on Whit Sunday, when church-going tended to be a fashion parade.

The photographs illustrate the changing fashions of those decades. In one of the Sunday School outing to Amesbury in 1912 or 1913 the ladies are smartly dressed in Edwardian costumes, and it is noteworthy that they are all in their Sunday best. Though many of them, and especially the children, travelled by farm waggon, the well-to-do probably went by pony and trap. Nor did the men make any concession to the summer weather. All are wearing their Sunday suits, complete with collar and tie, waistcoat and, in many instances, hard hat. Note the boys with their large white collars overlapping their jerkin-like jackets. Ten years later these were going out of fashion, but the author remembers having to wear such a collar, over a corduroy jacket, when attending primary school, and being laughed at for the difficulties he had in getting it fixed again when the stud came unfastened. Shirts with collars attached were refinements of the future. On workdays the men dispensed with the collars but always fastened the shirts at the neck with a brass stud.

The picture of a farmworker scuffing the soil with the toe of his boot illustrates also the typical footwear and legwear of those days. The corduroy trousers may also be seen in the photos of Ted Whitlock, though taken more than thirty years apart. In the nineteenth century directories James Barnett is entered as a bootmaker, and that is exactly what he was. He made boots, though he could turn his hand to repairing them as well. Note the button boots for the girls in the photo of Pitton school in the 1920s. And boots for the boys, too; no wellingtons yet.

In 1912 the older generation could remember when women wore pattens, which were a kind of overshoe with raised soles, to go to church or chapel on Sundays, as a protection against the prevalent mud.

By the time of the charabanc excursions to the seaside in the 1920s, fashions had changed a bit. The men are wearing caps and trilbys instead of hard hats, and for the ladies bucket hats are fashionable, though a beret and a few school caps are visible. Most of the party stick to convention, only one of the men daring to appear in an open-necked shirt. The charabanc driver smokes a cigarette, a decided innovation.

Women now in their seventies remember that they never had new 'shop' dresses until they were old enough to go to town, as teenagers, and buy them. Their mothers 'ran them up' on sewing-machines, which were part of the equipment taken for granted in most households, though in the late 1920s and 1930s buying by mail order became fashionable. Many of the older housewives, however, still used the carrier to do their shopping for clothes. Lewis White was well accustomed to taking discreet notes to the Salisbury drapers and bringing home the orders in brown paper parcels.

Flannel for underclothes was much in demand. The author, as a boy, was never allowed to go without a flannel shirt, winter and summer. When wearing an open-necked shirt for cricket, he had to have the high-necked flannel shirt underneath pinned back with a safety pin. Flannel shirts were mended and patched till they could bear no more. They were then cut up for face flannels.

To see his father wearing a flannel undershirt, a thick overshirt, corduroy breeches, thick woollen stockings, heavy boots and a waistcoat when working in the fields in summer weather struck young Ralph, after a time, as being a bit incongruous, but when he said as much, his father replied, 'Thick clothes keep out the heat in summer as well as keep it in in winter.' To some extent Ted was probably right, though it is also true that, in general, comfort ranked pretty low in our ancestors' priorities.

At some period in his teens the author staged a rebellion

against convention by wearing newly acquired pyjamas on a sweltering day in harvest, but he quickly learned his lesson. His job that day happened to be loading wheat-sheaves on waggons, and the hard sharp-edged straw and rough ears penetrated the thin pyjama fabric so thoroughly that his skin could not have been more raw if he had had measles.

It was not until he was ten or twelve that an inspector or health visitor at school impressed on the children the need for cleaning their teeth. This was an entirely new idea to him and indeed to the rest of his family, none of whom apparently had ever used a toothbrush. On the next visit to town his father duly came home with a toothbrush and the only toothpaste he had ever heard of – a tin of powdered charcoal. Young Ralph Whitlock obediently cleaned his teeth daily with the black powder for a few months until someone introduced him to Gibb's dentifrice.

Toilet rolls were another modern amenity unknown to the villagers. Newpaper, regardless of printers' ink, had to serve. It was, of course, a minor inconvenience in the business of going to the lavatory on a winter's night. The siting of the privy at the far end of the garden, though arranged to keep the edifice as far from the house as possible, had obvious disadvantages. The vulgar rhyme that children used to chant when they thought their parents weren't listening, though it would mean little to a modern child, described the experience graphically:

> Old King Cole was a merry old soul, and a merry old soul was he,
> He called for a light in the middle of the night to go to the WC.
> The way was long, the wind was strong, and the candle wouldn't fit.
> Old King Cole fell in the hole … [You can guess the rest of it].

Candles could be made to fit candlesticks by wrapping paper around the bottom, so that they stayed firm in the sockets without wobbling about. When candles of standard size were available at Aunt Polly's, there were seldom problems of that sort, but a previous generation had often had to manufacture their own candles, from sheep fat. This was strictly forbidden, it being feared that labourers might be tempted to kill a sheep, or at least to allow a sick one to die, in order to secure a supply of tallow. The fat had to be melted down surreptitiously, and old folk could remember when their fathers made expeditions at night to the river at Alderbury, there to cut the hollow stems of the big water dropwort, to be used as moulds for making candles.

11 Birth, Marriage, Sickness and Death

Information about how our more immediate ancestors regarded sex, pregnancy and birth control is hard to come by, for the reason that for the children of the 1920s and 1930s they were an impenetrable mystery. Suggestive jokes and smutty tales were told by men in the presence of boys who only half understood them. All around them animals and birds were mating and producing and rearing their young, but just how to translate all this in terms of human behaviour was tricky.

It would be satisfying to be able to record the existence of traditional methods of contraception, perhaps herbal, but enquiries have revealed nothing. The nearest approach to it was the occasional use of chewed hemp (long ago a farm crop and still surviving here and there as a farmyard weed) to procure an abortion. In the absence of hemp (another name for which is cannabis), green horse-radish leaves would do.

There was also a moribund belief in corpse money. This was a coin placed on the mouth of a person immediately after death, as a token payment for the sins of the deceased. Presumably the idea was derived from the very ancient custom of providing the dead person with a coin to pay the ferryman to take the soul across the Styx, but in village lore the payment was offered to the Devil. However, it was all very confusing, because the coin had to be removed before burial. It became the property of the woman who prepared the corpse for burial, and evidently in times past, though before our period, she would sometimes sell it for more than double its face value to any neighbour who decided she had had enough children. One supposes she carefully preserved the coin as a kind of talisman.

Not that in many families there was any desire to limit offspring. A common attitude was that the arrival of a new baby was an expected annual event in spring-time, like the flowering of the primroses and the coming of the swallows. Sarah Parsons, daughter of Joshua White, was not exceptional in producing a family of thirteen children.

Towards the end of the 1930s the village had, in theory at least, the services of a district nurse who lived four miles away at Alderbury, but this was of little practical value in an emergency before the installation of telephones (1938). Babies then, as now, had a habit of arriving at night, and every village had its unofficial midwife, who could be relied on to know what to do.

Although straightforward birth was a hurdle which a healthy country girl would normally take in her stride, there was little knowledge of how to cope with the unusual. Breech babies were a dangerous hazard, and puerperal fever claimed many a life.

Certain times of the year were unlucky for birth. Strangely, May was one of the unluckiest months, perhaps because in past centuries of fasts and famines a mother might well arrive at May in a half-starved and weakened state. The most unpopular season, however, was harvest time. An unfortunate child revealing that her birthday was in August would be forever pursued by the chant:

> Betty, Betty Jarvis,
> Come about in harvest.

Harvest was such a busy and vital matter that no one welcomed the distraction caused by the arrival of a new baby. Ted Whitlock, when gleaning, as a boy, with his mother in a harvest field, remembers one of the neighbours being absent for a day but arriving the next morning with a new baby which she made comfortable under a pile of sheaves.

Mortality at childbirth was matched by mortality in infancy and childhood. The saying that, in earlier times, 'A man's first illness was his last' was commonly repeated. It was held to refer to mature men but certainly it could have been widely applied to infants.

'When my mother was a girl,' said Alice Whitlock, 'you didn't ask a wife how many children she had *had*. You asked her how many she had *reared*.'

Most villagers now in their seventies can remember attending funerals of classmates, and some have memories of being pall-bearers. Mention has already been made of William Baugh, who recalled seeing three of his sisters lying dead together in the parlour of their cottage in the late nineteenth century. Sunday School hymns much in favour in the early part of our period dwelt somewhat morbidly (by our standards) on death, but death was a subject on which Edwardian children were well-informed. 'There's a home for little children, above the bright blue sky' and 'And there we shall with Jesus reign, and never, never part again.' were Sunday School favourites. In contrast to the attitudes of the late twentieth century, sex was a taboo subject but death was definitely not.

Dealing with childhood ailments devolved almost entirely on the mother, with the assistance of aunts, grandmothers and neighbours. The doctor was called in only as a last recourse and then usually too late, for those six miles between him and his patients were a forbidding barrier in the days before cars and telephones. Ted Whitlock relates that when his son Ralph was born, on a cold February night, he had to cycle to Salisbury to rouse the doctor, who had to dress, harness the horse and drive six miles over the dark, bleak hills. Almost needless to say, the baby was born long before he arrived.

Some villages possessed characters who had a local reputation as witches. In the nineteenth century Winterslow was the home of a celebrated witch, Lyddie Shears, who was said to exercise a powerful influence on her neighbours by the use of spells and similar arts. She was also in league with the local poachers.

'If they took Lyddie backy and snuff, she would go out with flint and steel striking sparks which attracted hares so that the poachers could knock them over. The legend is that she so teased a certain Farmer Turner by turning herself into a hare for him to course with his greyhounds, the hare always disappearing in her garden, that the farmer sought the advice of the rector of West Tytherley. The good man recommended that a bullet be made of a sixpenny-piece. The farmer with it shot the elusive hare, and the witch was found dead in her cottage with a silver bullet in her heart!'

It is a good story but one which hardly bears investigation. Is it likely that a post-mortem was carried out to reveal the bullet?

In fact, the tale of a witch being shot by a silver bullet is attributed to localities in many different parts of England, and the association of hares with witchcraft is very ancient. What probably happened is that Winterslow villagers, by some means hearing of these matters, associated them with their local witch and rounded them off to form a neat story.

Although Winterslow claimed other alleged witches much later than Lyddie Shears – right down to the 1930s, in fact – Pitton seems to have had none. The knowledge of herbal medicine and even of medical magic was, however, widespread. Almost every household possessed a medicine cupboard stocked with remedies against winter ills. By the 1930s the mail-order business had extended into the realm of proprietary medicines, and most families seem to have stocked Beecham's powders, Burgess's Lion ointment and Box's indigestion pills. Between them these three panaceas took care of most ailments, though colds, coughs and chest complaints were best dealt with by herbal infusions. One of the most efficacious was mint tea, taken piping hot just before going to bed. Raspberry tea, made from an infusion of raspberry leaves, was held to be equally effective in treating fevers.

Some of the most troublesome complaints have now fortunately become uncommon. Chilblains, for instance, seem to have affected most people in winter, though some more drastically than others. Kate Whitlock suffered torments every winter from chilblains on her ears. She and her sister-in-law, Alice, made an ointment of ground holly berries mixed with goose fat, if obtainable, otherwise with lard. Kate rubbed this on her ears but the correct method of using the ointment on toes and fingers was to smear it liberally on the affected part, wrap it tightly in an old worsted stocking and toast the limbs in front of a fire until the heat became unbearable. From present-day knowledge of the complaint and its causes, it would seem that the treatment probably made it worse.

Styes on the eyes were another formerly common misfortune which seems to have become rare. Treatment was also with Lion ointment or with goose fat. The latter was, in fact, very much in demand as an almost universal panacea. Many a child wore a poultice of goose fat spread on flannel on his or her chest for the greater part of the winter.

The prime example of folk remedies concerns warts, with which previous generations seem to have been remarkably preoccupied. The treatment for warts falls into three or four main categories. The most numerous involves rubbing the juices of certain plants on the wart, the dandelion, milk-thistle, greater celandine, mullein, house-leak, St John's wort, petty spurge and hart's-tongue fern being examples. In the second category are certain caustic and similar substances, such as washing soda, ashes of willow bark mixed with vinegar, mother-o'-pearl buttons dissolved in lemon juice, raw meat, teazel roots boiled in wine, and the blood of mole, rat or cat.

Anomalous remedies are the soft, downy lining of broad bean pods, a hot pin stuck into the centre of the wart (very painful, one would imagine!), fasting spittle, meaning saliva before one's mouth has been rinsed out in the morning, and a sheet cobweb, which later has to be burned.

The moon featured quite prominently in local folklore. It was generally believed that changes in the weather were heralded by the phases of the moon. The cottage pig had always to be killed when the moon was waxing; if the moon was waning, the bacon would shrink. Almost all seeds must likewise be sown during a waxing moon, with the exception of broad beans.

It was unlucky to view a new moon through glass, and many women would insist on being warned when a new moon was visible, so that they could step outside and not have their first sight of it through a window. One lady who always followed this practice nevertheless kept her glasses on! To sleep with moonlight shining on one's face was both unlucky and sure to bring bad dreams. Indeed, it was unlucky for the moon to shine on one's face at any time. Alice Whitlock (née White) used to laugh about her mother, Julia, who, when a young woman, always carried a parasol when walking through the woods on a moonlit night. The ridiculous aspect of the situation appealed to Alice, but Julia was doubtless following an ancient convention.

Against all these unfavourable omens, however, can be set the belief that for the harvest moon to shine on the bed of a newly married couple on their wedding night was a sure token of a long and happy married life.

A thunderstorm on a wedding day was held to presage a stormy life for the newly married couple, or, according to one version, a childless marriage. On the other hand, a child conceived during a thunderstorm would be strong and healthy. During a thunderstorm, too, a nursing mother would never suckle her baby, as it was held that the milk would curdle in its stomach.

On the onset of thunder a prudent housewife would cover with cloths any mirrors or bright metal objects which, it was thought, would attract the lightning. She would also open both front and back doors so that any 'thunderbolt' which entered the house, through a door or down the chimney, would quickly roll out again. It was considered unlucky to burn logs from trees which had been struck by lightning.

Should a thunderstorm happen when a coffin lay in a house, another death would occur within a year. No mother would buy, borrow or accept as a gift a perambulator or a cradle that had been occupied by a baby who had died. Sundry omens were interpreted as foretelling death. A cat leaving a house where someone lay sick or a robin entering it foretold the imminence of death. When the use of candles was commonplace, a guttering candle producing a whorl of melted wax was said to be making a coffin handle. Or a candle which set strips of molten wax running down the sides was thought to be fashioning a shroud.

As soon as possible after a death the mourning bell was tolled at the church. Most older residents of the village can remember when Walter White, the sexton, performed this service. Workers in the fields would stop work for a minute to listen to the message of the bells – one sombre note for a man, two for a woman, three for a child. They could usually conjecture who had passed away, for they were always well informed about anyone who was seriously ill.

The last services to the corpse, including washing it, dressing it in a shroud and preparing it for burial were usually, in Pitton, performed in the 1920s and 1930s by Emily Mills, a very practical and efficient housewife.

Immediately a death occurred, all the blinds in the house were drawn, and on the day of the funeral all blinds were drawn in houses passed by the procession. A widow normally dressed in black – 'widow's weeds' – for at least a year after her husband's death, and many of the older women never wore any other colour. Men wore black, and even children had black arm-bands. Some families still preserve mourning cards, printed in black and decorated with silver lilies or crosses and bearing the name of the deceased, with details of age and date of death and perhaps a religious verse or text. Notepaper edged in black was customarily used for personal correspondence for a period after the death. Black-edged handkerchiefs and black necklaces were also not unknown.

On the day of the funeral work generally stopped in the village for an hour or so. Anyone not intimately connected with the family or attending the funeral would stand still and raise his hat when the cortège passed. The funeral procession moved at a slow walking pace, but no one would ever dream of overtaking it. Apart from the matter of disrespect, people would say that he was hurrying to his own grave.

12 The Years of Change

When Owen Griffin, speaking at the village celebration of the Jubilee of King George V in 1935, said, 'When we look around at our village today and remember it as it used to be, we realize that no previous generation has ever seen such changes as we have seen,' he was making what seemed to him and his audience a reasonable statement.

True, plenty of previous generations would have challenged it. The generation that lived through the trauma of the Enclosure Acts, for instance. The generation that experienced civil war. The generation that saw ecclesiastical landowners replaced by new-rich profit-hunters. The generation that suffered the Black Death.

The generation that endured the Norman Conquest. And many other earlier generations.

Nevertheless the generation that spanned the period from the Victorian Age through the Edwardian to the landmark of George V's twenty-fifth year had had to exercise more than normal adaptability, even though to subsequent generations, who have had to cope with a succession of yet more traumatic changes, it may seem a time of relative tranquillity. The village of 1912, the year of the Sale, was by 1935 fast fading into oblivion.

The new order established by the changes resulting from the Sale (though it was not immediately so very different from the old) had only three years to settle down before it was shaken by the cataclysm of war. Few of those old enough to remember that first world war still survive. Their memories are of the men who came back and of what their fathers and uncles told them. Casualties from Pitton were mercifully few, and a good number of conscripted soldiers came back to the village and resumed their former way of life. Owen Griffin, who spent several years as a prisoner-of-war and who married after his return, the brothers Ernest, Percy and Sid Whitlock, unrelated Vic Whitlock, Alex Pearce, Lew Mills, Willoughby Talbot, Fred and Sid Collins, and Len Noyce are among the names recorded.

Ernest and Percy Whitlock returned from the war to work on the land, Ernest afterwards becoming a farmer. Sid became the village roadman. Alec Pearce started his own builder's business. Willoughby Talbot continued his career as a schoolmaster. Owen Griffin, townbred, came to Pitton to carve a new career for himself as a farmer. Vic Whitlock worked on the farm for his cousin Ted and afterwards started his own market gardening business. Lew Mills took a job at an Army establishment on Salisbury Plain. So the record goes on, a record of solid character and sterling adaptability.

The interests of the village continued to be overwhelmingly agricultural, so events in the farming world had their inevitable repercussions. In 1922 the Corn Production Act, with its implied guarantee of a modicum of prosperity for agriculture, was repealed. Britain had grown rich by its exports of manufactured goods, in which it led the world, and a critical factor in the equation was the availability of cheap food for the factory workers. Food could now be imported more cheaply than it could be grown in the fields of England, and the shipping required helped in the nation's prosperity. Against all that, home agriculture was an expendable pawn. It was as simple as that.

Ted Whitlock put down 1924, the year in which he took over Webb's Farm from Will Clark, as the last year of adequate farming prosperity. History records the Great Depression as beginning in 1926, but on British farms it started two years earlier. Land went derelict, hedges grew unkempt, bankruptcies multiplied. Sheep virtually disappeared from the ideal grazing country of the Wiltshire downs. Their place was taken by millions of rabbits, in spite of trapping, snaring, shooting and ferreting. Nothing made much impression on the proliferating hordes until the introduction of myxomatosis in 1953.

With the departure of the sheep, one of the chief markets of the underwood workers, who cut hazel rods for hurdles, dwindled and all but vanished. The era of the woodland craftsmen thus came to an end, after centuries – perhaps millennia – of existence, though a few practitioners have kept the old lore alive to the present day.

When the search for another livestock enterprise to succeed the uneconomic sheep alighted, as it was almost bound to, on cows, the village farmers had a lot to learn. In the first place, there was custom and prejudice to be overcome. The great sheep farmers of the chalk downs tended to look down on the cow-keepers as mere 'teat-pullers'. True, most of them kept a house cow or two, to supply the farmhouse, farmworkers and a few of the neighbours with milk (and in some instances with butter or cheese), but usually some old codger, past heavier work, had the job of milking twice a day. There were no milk deliveries, of course. Milk had to be fetched in jug or milk-can from the farmhouse door.

Cows were mongrel, nondescript animals. The work of

Bakewell, the great eighteenth-century pioneer of live-stock breeding, 150 years earlier, was unheard of in these parts. In general, however, the cows were, loosely, of Shorthorn breed and were chosen for their colour rather than for any other quality. The title of A.G. Street's book *Strawberry Roan* described the general preference, a good light or reddish roan. The trouble was that, years earlier, the Shorthorn breed had split into two sections, one concentrating on beef and the other on dairy. Farmers who had pedigree herds and selected rigidly for type were safe enough, but the rank-and-file had no guide as to whether the cow they liked the look of had dairying qualities or just used all her food to create flesh. It didn't matter under the old dispensation; you milked the cow as long as she produced milk and then sold her for beef, so any loss on one count was compensated for by the other. Now, however, the new dairy farmers had to consider economic milk production, and the cattle markets of the day could offer them little guidance.

In Salisbury farmers in search of dairy-type cows tended to favour New Forest cattle. These were traditionally based on Guernsey or Jersey cows but had been at times reinforced by bulls, known among farmers as Isigny bulls, imported from Normandy. They stamped their progeny with easily recognized brindling. The Channel Island crossbreds were certainly more reliable than the Short-horns, though their prime feature was the production of quality milk, rich in cream, rather than quantity.

It was the unreliability of the dominant Shorthorn types, however, which gave the black-and-white Friesians, imported from the Netherlands and established as a recognized breed in 1909, their chance. They did not appear in Pitton herds, however, until the late 1930s.

With the advent of commercial cows, the problem of keeping a bull or bulls arose. At first some farmers kept their own bull, a nice-looking animal of their own breeding, chosen, as usual, solely for its appearance. Later, there seems to have arisen a tacit understanding on keeping a village bull, the farmer who invested in one charging service fees. At one time, when Owen Griffin kept the village bull at Parsonage Farm, it caused some embarrassment to the schoolteachers, as the yard in which the mating took place was overlooked by the school windows. When the author, then living at Webb's Farm, was custodian of the village bull, his own inclinaton was to ignore any of his father's cows which came into season on Sundays or holidays, but most of the other farmers were less considerate, and it seemed to him that Christmas Day always brought a procession of cows needing the bull.

Another specialization which flourished with the coming of the commercial cows was the village cattle cart, property of Luther White. It was a kind of tumbril, low-slung on the axle and drawn by a quiet old horse. The calf or calves rode in the cart, which was low enough for the cow, following behind, to see and touch it, and so she was encouraged to walk the six miles to Salisbury. The cattle cart was the only feasible method of getting a cow to or from market. Ted Whitlock's men were once required to drive seven or eight heifers to Salisbury, over the downs, but they tried it only once. The men were exhausted before the cattle were, and were in no mood to deal with irate suburban householders who had left their garden gates open.

The market for milk was provided by the United Dairies, which had a depot in Salisbury, whither the Pitton farmers went once a year to make the best bargain they could. The innovation which made the whole business possible was the introduction of motor traffic. At some time early in the 1920s Lionel White, whose father Lewis had operated the last carrier's cart, bought a lorry and set up a milk-transport business. The milk was collected in churns from all the local farms and delivered to the depot in Salisbury.

The trade and the size of the herds gradually increased, as was happening all over the country, paving the way for the establishment, in 1933, of the Milk Marketing Board. From then on, farmers were at least working to a known contract, with prices fixed annually, though of course at a level lower than they wanted. Gradually, too, hygiene was improved and the principles of genetic selection were disseminated, resulting in a slow improvement in the quality of the dairy cattle. Artificial insemination, however, was not introduced, at least locally, until after the Second World War.

In the early 1930s motor traffic was also making it possible for people other than farmworkers to live in isolated houses, and these newcomers offered a new market for farm and garden produce. Ted Whitlock was in the right position to take advantage of it, for he already had a produce round in Salisbury.

It happened this way. At the time of his marriage, in 1901, to Alice, the youngest daughter of Joshua White of Church Farm. Ted was earning ten shillings a week, catching rabbits on the Clarendon estate. Casual work occupied the winter months, but in spring and summer he returned to the more skilled work of shearing, trimming and preparing sheep for sales and fairs. He and his uncle and cousin were the right-hand men of the auctioneers who were carving for themselves a niche in the agricultural world. Often he was away from home for weeks on end.

At home Alice grew bored. Like many village girls of the time, she had 'gone into service', starting at Salisbury but soon migrating to London and finishing up in the exalted post of parlourmaid. In that career she was required to do little work but to look smart and presentable in the uniform provided. These domestic servants, especially those so high in the hierarchy, behaved as ladies when they returned on holiday from the metropolis, which the young men naturally found most attractive but the stay-at-home women noticeably disapproved.

However, it was not long after her marriage before Alice reverted to type. Cycling to Salisbury, she made contact with some of the ladies for whom she had once worked. Friendships sprang up, and soon she was cycling to town once a week, her bicycle laden with butter, eggs, dressed chicken, fruit and other produce from the farm. She was, in fact, following much the same business as her father had engaged in before he became a farmer.

By the following autumn she had developed such a round of customers that she was bringing into the house almost as much cash as her husband. When winter came and with it the casual scarcity of work, Ted joined forces with her, and so two loaded bicycles were pushed to market once or twice a week. The business prospered to such an extent that they invested in a New Forest pony and trap, which in due course were succeeded by a Ford one-ton van, as recounted earlier.

As the 1920s wore on, motor traffic multiplied on the still inadequate roads and encouraged settlement in previously uninhabited areas. Villagers who were children then remember taking Sunday evening walks with their parents to the London road ('the turnpike') to see if any cars were on the road!

In due course, two garages (Clearway and Haven) were opened by immigrants from London, to be followed shortly by a few more tentative houses or huts which were ere long to develop into a flood of settlement. These represented new, ready-made markets for Ted, and one of the first demands they made was for fresh milk. So Ted obliged, first carrying the milk in lidded buckets from which he ladled it out as required. Later, in the 1930s, he switched to bottling milk, filling the bottles by hand in the dairy at White Hill and washing them in the kitchen sink. It was time-consuming work but more rewarding than selling milk wholesale.

Most of the Pitton farmers in these years also increased their stock of poultry, especially of laying hens, there being an expanding market for eggs.

Crop yields, incidentally, were abysmally low, by present standards. The farmers were reasonably content if they harvested 30 cwt of wheat or barley per acre and delighted if their crop gave two tons. Sometimes the income from the rabbits killed when the corn was cut was as large as that from the grain itself. The straw, however, was a bonus, needed as litter for the cows.

Farming continued to be based on manual labour, labour-saving devices being still in the future. Certainly the corn was cut by a horse-drawn binder and the hay by a horse-drawn grass-cutter, but hand labour was the rule for most other jobs, and even for harvesting corn a swathe as wide as the binder had to be mown by scythe, to allow the binder to pass without damaging the grain.

The sheaves thrown out by the binder had to be picked up by hand and stood in tent-shaped hiles, to dry. In a dry summer four or five days in the field were sufficient for this process, but in a wet season the hiles might have to be dismantled, the sheaves turned and the hiles rebuilt several times. Under the worst conditions the string binding the sheaves might have to be cut, the straw thrown out to dry and then handled loosely by prong, like hay.

Grass cut for hay was allowed to lie on the ground for a few days, then turned by a horse-drawn machine known as a side rake. When adequately dried, it was collected into twisted heaps (pooks) by workers with two-grained prongs.

Both pooks of hay and sheaves of corn were pitched onto waggons by men with two-grained prongs and transported to the rickyard. Traditionally this should have been at the rear of the farmyard, but the unusual arrangement of the Pitton farms decreed that the ricks were generally built at field corners. Rick-building was a highly skilled task, usually undertaken by the farmer himself, though some farmers were more proficient than others. Ricks which needed to be propped up by poles invited ridicule, but there were plenty of them.

Harvest was a community event. For a full team working at carting sheaves a farmer needed at least seven men, with a boy to lead the horses as they hauled the waggons to and from the rick. Simultaneously, cutting the corn in another field might well be in progress, which required the services of a skilled carter with another team of horses and any number of old men, women and children shaping the sheaves into hiles. And every farmer in the village would be engaged in harvesting at the same time. Therefore, as the corn ripened and the binder blades were sharpened, an urgent recruiting campaign was launched. Schoolmaster, baker, roadman, carpenters, thatcher, bricklayers, pensioners, boys and girls – every available hand was pressed into service.

As recently as the 1890s the village women, especially widows and other poor folk, had gleaned in the harvest fields, picking up shed ears of corn for their own use. By the beginning of our period the pressing need seems to have passed, but during the 1914-18 war women were needed for jobs which they had never before undertaken. The younger ones learned how to handle prongs like professionals and tackled all the harvest jobs which had formerly been reserved for men. The emancipation of women had begun.

The scythe, that most satisfying of all hand-tools, was, since the introduction of the binder, reserved for small tasks, such as the cutting of awkward corners of fields and preparing a track for binders and grasscutters. Most farmers and farmworkers were, however, still adept at using it. A good scythe-man could cut an acre of corn a day and took a pride in doing so. Using a scythe is a skill that needs much practice, for the secret is to swing it with the body, not to employ chopping motions. In times past a skilled practitioner with the scythe could mow a lawn almost as closely as can be achieved with a modern lawn-mower. Chopping was the role of the reap-hook, another much valued tool, used for cutting hedges, nettles and similar tidying-up. Billhooks were for cutting bushes, hazel rods and general underwood work and especially for use in hedging. Bidles (presumably a corruption of 'beetles') were heavy-headed wooden mallets for knocking in fence-posts. The head was supposed always to be of dried apple wood. The thatcher had a set of hand-made tools of his own, fashioned by himself. The shepherd treasured his crook.

The farm tool most frequently in use apart from the prong was the hoe. It represented the only weapon the farmers had against weeds, in a war waged incessantly throughout the growing season. Many of the independent or self-employed villagers spent the winter months working in the woods and the summer on the farm, hoeing. Horse-hoes had recently been introduced for inter-row work in turnip fields.

Although the seed drill had been invented, by Jethro

Tull, in 1701, it had found a place on only a few of the Pitton farms at the beginning of the period. Several men still living can remember being set to sow seed broadcast by hand, carrying the seed in a 'seed-lip' – a container made to fit neatly around the body. This was hard work, as the sower was required to tramp over roughly ploughed fields. Even worse, – much worse – was the sowing of sulphate of ammonia, which apparently was introduced to the Pitton farms in the 1920s or early 1930s. It came in a crystallized form like salt and was sown by hand from a seed-lip. Naturally it made the skin raw after a time. The author remembers going on strike against the practice and insisting that the alternative, of shovelling the stuff from the tail-end of a cart, should be substituted.

An item of barn equipment that used to be passed around from farm to farm was a winnowing machine. Its purpose was to clean grain in order to obtain a good sample for sowing, which reveals yet another shortcoming of farming in that period. Few farmers purchased seed grain, preferring to use their own or to exchange with their neighbours. Textbooks state that during these decades Red Standard and Squarehead's Master were the dominant wheat varieties in England, but the Pitton farmers doubtfully knew those names. Wheat was just wheat, and you didn't spend good money on seed if you could use your own.

All the older farms possessed a barn with a threshing floor. This was the central section of a large building, often larger than the farmhouse, with other compartments of equal size on either side. In every instance the central compartment had a solid board floor, built to withstand the hammering of flails. Before the introduction of steam threshing-engines, threshing with flails provided winter work for many agricultural labourers. The compartments on either side of the floor were piled to the rafters with sheaves, either stored there at harvest or fetched by waggon from the rickyard at intervals. The threshing floor had two sets of double doors, as broad as the floor and reaching to the eaves, so that a waggon could draw up on either side. Sacks of corn went out on one side, and loose straw on the other.

Some of the Pitton barns were older than their attendant farmhouses. All were thatched, and in some of them the great oak timbers had evidently been used time and again. Old mortices and tenons were to be seen in places where now they served no useful purpose. Some were said to be ships' timbers, which seems likely enough, for the port of Southampton lies only twenty miles away. On a beam in the old barn at Bowers Farm a seventeeth-century date had been carved.

Flails were, incidentally, still to be seen in some barns in the 1920s but few of the farmers or labourers had ever used one. Old William Baugh confessed that he had tried and had nearly knocked himself out. Apparently in unskilled hands the loose arm of the flail had a knack of coming up behind the wielder and catching him a clout on the back of the head. Threshing with flails was tiring, dusty work (though probably no dustier than threshing by steam-engine), as vividly described in an earlier century by Stephen Duck, the Wiltshire thresher poet, but its replacement by the threshing-machine was vigorously opposed. The memory of the Machinery Riots of 1830, triggered by the introduction of the new threshing-machines, still lingered nearly a hundred years later – doubtless with reason, for south Wiltshire was in the heart of the disturbances, and many families in Pitton and neighbouring villages lost men and boys sentenced to transportation to Australia.

From time to time in the autumns and winters of the 1920s and 1930s steam-driven threshing-engines used to arrive to thresh the farmers' corn-ricks. Each farm then experienced a hectic few days, and there was much neighbourly co-operation, for few farms could muster a sufficient team to keep a threshing-machine going. The threshing-machine gang generally consisted of the driver (usually the man who owned the outfit), a man to cut the sheaves and feed them into the drum, and sometimes a boy. The farmer was expected to provide two or three men to dismantle the rick and throw the sheaves to the feeder, two more to build a rick of the threshed straw, and another to undertake the excessively dusty job of 'minding the chaff and caven'. The farmer himself generally dealt with the threshed grain, tying the sacks as they filled and wheeling them aside on sack-trucks. The carter hauled the grain to the barn and kept the threshing-engine supplied with coal and water. Altogether threshing was a formidable and exhausting interruption to the farm routine, and everyone was glad when it was over, though the farmer of course had compensation in sacks of grain for sale.

Another building considered essential on old-time farms, though somewhat neglected by the 1920s, was the granary. This was a thatched, cube-shaped box perched on staddle-stones, for protection against rats and mice. In theory, of course, the vermin were prevented from entering by the mushroom overhang, but by the 1930s too often the object of the staddle-stones had been forgotten and nullified by deposits of junk which offered a highway to rodents. Inside, the granary had a central aisle with board boxes on either side, enabling the several types of grain to be stored separately. Spare compartments were sometimes used for storing apples.

Attached to the barn or stable, quite often as a lean-to (especially when corrugated iron came into common use), was a cart-shed. Here were housed the two wheeled tip-carts found on every farm and the farm waggons. These, locally made, were of two main types. The common ones had a flat bottom with no sides but detachable end-ladders. A more sophisticated and elaborate design was the boat-waggon, which had sides eighteen inches high, supporting benches which overhung the wheels and on which, on occasion, passengers could perch. The moveable ladders with which both types were equipped enabled them to be loaded high with sheaves, but with the boat-waggon it was possible for an expert (Ted Mills was outstanding) to build a 'swan-back' load which could climb to a height of four or five feet above the waggon bed without benefit of ladders.

Most farmers appreciated the value of carts and waggons sufficiently to park them under cover, but they had less regard for other machinery. Binders were generally covered with a tarpaulin or rick-cloth and were accorded a place in a shed if space could be found. Otherwise they spent their idle time under a hedge, together with grass-mower, ploughs, horse-hoes, harrows, rollers and other accessories. Cutting blades were, however, removed after use and stored indoors.

By present-day financial standards, Pitton farmers of the 1920s and 1930s were unbelievably poor. Prices paid for property at the 1911 Sale have been forgotten, but in 1924 a farm of about forty-five acres, with a small farmhouse and buildings, changed hands for £400. Farm workers' cottages were thrown in at around £50 a pair. Rents for farmland were at the rate of five shillings to ten shillings an acre, including house and buildings.

Under a benign ruling by the Inland Revenue, though doubtless initiated to save the Tax Office work, the rental value of a farm was held to be equivalent to the farmer's income. In poverty-stricken Pitton, no farm had a rental value of £100, and most considerably less. It follows that no one in Pitton was deemed to have an annual income of £100 or more, which consigned the village to a contemptible limbo, beneath the notice of the Tax Inspector. In consequence, few farmers bothered to keep any accounts, apart from a ledger recording debts and credits.

Farmworkers' wages at the beginning of the period were around £1 a week, rising later to thirty shillings. The farmer's own income was, in most instances, no higher. The farmer and his men worked side by side and mingled socially on equal terms. There was no class barrier or class consciousness. How could there be, when nearly everybody was related anyway? It was an egalitarian economy, based on poverty, though not on deprivation. Nobody had any money worth speaking of, but no one went hungry.

One incident from those years serves to illustrate the prevailing attitude to village property. In 1934 an area of derelict land on the far side of Piccadilly Clump, in Winterbourne parish, came up for sale on the death of its owner, a retired Salisbury brewer who had been interested only in its sporting rights. The 230 acres of derelict fields, scrub and downland were offered to Ted Whitlock for £750 the lot. Ted went straight to a Salisbury bank and asked for a loan to buy it. He offered as collateral the deeds of his four-bedroomed house and buildings. The bank manager laughed at him.

'You call that security? In a place like Pitton? If you want to waste your money,' he added, 'go and do it on women or horses, not on that worthless stuff. But you don't waste mine!'

So Ted persuaded the neighbouring Clarendon estate to buy the land, at the stipulated £750, and to let it to him at two shillings an acre annually. For the first few years he paid the rent with rabbits, which swarmed there. Later, on the approach of war, he began to reclaim some of the derelict fields, and during the war the neglected acres were all brought back into cultivation and produced worthwhile crops.

Although farmers failed to recognize it at the time, the most important agricultural development of the 1920s and 1930s was the vastly increased availability of chemical fertilizers, pioneered by sulphate of ammonia and then followed closely by basic slag, superphosphate and kainit. Compound fertilizers came later. Their advantage lay in the ease of transport. Since the foundering of the traditional sheep-and-corn system of farming, the upland fields were virtually out of bounds. Carting farmyard manure, by horse and cart, to the remoter fields was prohibitively expensive, even in those days of cheap labour, and so the far fields fell derelict. Sacks of chemical fertilizers offered a potential method of reclaiming them, and this was the method primarily used in the great war effort of the 1940s.

The introduction of the farm tractor attracted much more attention, for it was an era of mechanical madness. However, the tractor came relatively late in the period, Ted Whitlock being the first Pitton farmer to acquire one, in 1934. It was an iron-wheeled Fordson with strakes, which needed to be fitted with road-bands every time it was taken on the road. For the next few years after it came to the farm every form of ingenuity had to be brought into play to adapt the old horse-drawn implements for use with the tractor. Waggons, carts, seed-drills, binders and grass-cutters all had to be fitted with iron draw-bars, made in the smithy by Len Kerley. Until the war, however, the tractor was an auxiliary; most of the farm work was still powered by horses.

Through all these years of change agriculture wallowed in deep depression. The adoption of new ideas and techniques was long delayed by lack of finance and by the doubt, almost the certainty, that any improvements would be financially not worth while. After Ted Whitlock had acquired, as a tenant, the downland farm which he had vainly sought to buy, he determined to try cultivating a little of it. Selecting an area which had obviously once been ploughland (perhaps in Napoleonic times) he ploughed and sowed twenty acres with barley. The crop proved satisfactory as far as yields were concerned, but in the meantime the price of barley had fallen to half its level in the previous year, and so he sustained a substantial loss.

This must have been in 1936 or 1937, and any further reclamation had to wait until the exigencies of war demanded it. Even then doubt and discouragement prevailed. The official ploughing-up campaign, designed to produce as much food as possible from the fields of Britain, at first excluded the derelict downland as being not worth ploughing. Ted had to fight quite hard to get the ploughing-up grant of £2 an acre. As it proved, the soil was highly productive, or could be made so by the use of the new chemical fertilizers. It produced good crops not only of wheat, oats and barley but also of kale, turnips, potatoes and flax.

Through all the vicissitudes, life continued more or less unchanged on the peasant farms of Pitton. The cows trudged home daily to be milked; horse-ploughs ploughed most of the acres; in autumn the landscape was studded with hiles of sheaves; hedges became overgrown tangles threatening to smother the lanes.

Lack of cash for investment, and the absence of information about what was available, were presumably the reasons for the failure of any of the village farmers to instal milking-machines. They all plodded along with the familiar hand-milking. In the 1930s A.J. Hosier, a farmer of Wexcombe, near Marlborough, invented the portable milking bail – a shed on wheels which could be drawn around fields far from the farmstead, thus enabling those fields to be grazed by cows. The new petrol engines devised for motor cars could also be adapted to power milking-machines in these bails. Hosier brought into effective production big areas of chalk downland in his locality and was highly praised for his innovations and enterprise. But, although he lived only forty miles away, his achievements do not appear to have become known in Pitton until the 1940s, or at least they were not emulated.

One invention which was, however, almost universally adopted and with often deplorable results, was barbed wire. Evidently perfected in the trench warfare of the 1914-18 war, it was soon in use everywhere. It provided the perfect material for mending gaps in hedges, thus giving farmers an excuse for avoiding proper hedge maintenance. The countryside soon assumed the appearance of a series of barbed wire entanglements, with sad effects on the scenery. From a practical viewpoint, however, it did make possible the enclosure and hence exploitation of large areas of hitherto unfenced downland – an important consideration in wartime, though anathema to the climate of opinion in the 1980s.

When the author was asked, in a radio show, what he considered the invention that had had the most beneficial effect on country life, he replied, 'Wellington boots.' A good case could be made out of this contention. The heavy cobbler-made boots and gaiters which were the universal footwear in the early years of the century were in the 1920s and 1930s almost entirely banished in favour of rubber boots, to the profound contentment of the wearers.

Ted Whitlock's claim to have owned the first bicycle, other than a penny-farthing, ever to be seen in Pitton has already been mentioned. By the first decade of the twentieth century bicycles had become commonplace enough for it to be thought nothing out of the ordinary for Alice to ride to Salisbury each week, her bicycle laden with produce. Elderly men and women still living can recall seeing the first motor vehicles pass through Pitton, but after the First World War the numbers of motor cars quickly multiplied. Reg Bell acquired his bus, Lionel White his milk lorry, Ted Whitlock his ton Ford van, Alfred Bell a neat little tourer (make unremembered), Will Clark one of the earliest Austin 7s.

Motor-bikes, being within the financial reach of many young men, were naturally even more popular than motor cars. Indulgent mothers allowed either their cottage parlours or their kitchens (according to just how indulgent they were) to be used for dismantling motor-bikes on winter evenings. Remembering that oil lamps and candles were still the only available form of lighting, the hazards of inspecting leaks in petrol tanks by candle-light can be readily imagined, and such disasters as occurred can be considered inevitable. So too were the increasing numbers of traffic accidents. One particularly horrific episode when young Howard Horner, of Winterslow, was killed in crashing his motor-bike on the London road is still remembered.

When the responsibility for the upkeep of the country roads was taken over, in 1928, from the parish council by the County Council, little change occurred for the first few years. Sid Whitlock, the roadman, carried on filling in pot-holes and ruts with flints from the fields. By degrees, however, new road-making techniques were applied, and granite chippings gradually replaced the flints. A steam-driven road-roller appeared (the first on 27 March 1931, according to an extant diary), breaking the monopoly of the steam threshing-engine and adding to the anxieties of roadside cottagers with thatched roofs.

As already mentioned, the author, when starting his secondary education at Bishop Wordsworth's School in Salisbury, made the daily journey by bicycle. Two years later he was joined by Vivian Talbot, Willoughby Talbot's eldest son, but these two were the last of the Pitton boys to have to rely on pedal-pushing. Their younger brothers and cousins (and very soon afterwards, their sisters, for in 1927 Salisbury's new Grammar School for Girls opened) were able to travel by bus. The eight o'clock morning bus service, operated by Reg Bell, also opened new horizons for the villagers. Suddenly employment in the village fields or workshops and, for girls, going into domestic service were no longer the only options. The shops, hotels, garages and warehouses of the city beckoned, and Pitton started on the road to becoming a dormitory for commuters.

For the first decade, however, the traffic was almost entirely one-way. Pitton had discovered the town, but the town had not discovered Pitton. Remember the answer given in 1934 by the bank manager to Ted Whitlock when the latter applied for a loan, offering his four-bedroomed house in the village as security: 'Pitton? Who wants to saddle himself with property in a place like Pitton?' The installation of electricity, piped water and a telephone service were needed to change that attitude, and they did not arrive until 1938.

In fact, the village became familiar with radio ('wireless' was the word universally used) before the telephone. There was a local tradition that Marconi conducted some of his early experiments on the downs near Pitton. Will Clark and his two sons, Will and Stanley, were among the earliest village enthusiasts. As early as 1922 they were experimenting with crystal sets, and friends were frequently invited in on winter evenings to don head-phones and listen to the music and voices, though subject to much crackling and distortion, brought into the living-room by the new marvel. A little later, one of the much-appreciated services made possible by the steadily improving bus service was the collection and delivery of acid batteries for the village wireless sets.

Yet another service provided by the bus was the supply of daily papers. For the first time daily newspapers were available to the villagers. A batch was brought from Salisbury by the bus every morning and dropped at the shop, from where it was distributed to customers' doors. For Pitton communication was really being established with the world outside the parish boundaries.

*

When the New Inn, by Pitton Green, was flourishing in the middle years of the nineteenth century, it was apparently a centre of a colourful social life. On the opposite side of the road stood a skittle alley, a rather surprising amenity, for there is no widespread tradition of skittles in the district, and no one in the early twentieth century could recall ever indulging in the game. However, it seems that the alley was in its time a rendezvous for the village youths, concerning whom certain lurid escapades were related, such as firing a candle from a muzzle-loading gun through an inch plank and conducting various experiments with gunpowder and a blacksmith's anvil.

Long before the end of the century the New Inn and its skittle alley had vanished, and the new rendezvous for the village teenagers was an old stable at the far end of The Green. It rejoiced in the status of the village Reading Room, though very little reading went on there – rather, it was the scene of frequent horseplay and the general rowdiness associated with teenagers. The older and more sober elements of the community found comfort in the fact that the Reading Room was on the fringe of the village, where respectable citizens could ignore what was going on.

At some time in the first decade or so of the twentieth century 'The Old Stable' was acquired as a building site. The building was demolished and its place taken by Glebe House. This left the village with no centre for social activities, either respectable or otherwise.

From the point of view of enthusiastic chapel-goers, there was much to be said for that arrangement, for it left the chapel with a clear field and no competition. Many young people attended services on Sunday evenings, sitting in the back seats and carving their initials on the pews, for want of anything better to do. However, after the war a proposal that a new village hall or Reading Room should be erected instead of a war memorial (seeing that most of the village men who went to war came back unscathed) proved very popular. With public subscription, a disused Army hut was purchased, and it was erected by local labour.

The village had a social centre again. It was a simple timber hut with a galvanized iron roof. At one end was a stage, capable of being dismantled and re-erected with some ease. Behind it were two small rooms, used for preparing teas or as changing-rooms for concerts, and at the very rear some basic lavatories. Heat in winter was supplied by a solid-fuel 'Tortoise' stove, as at the school and the chapel. Someone presented the Reading Room with a piano; someone else contributed a dart board, a billiard table and a table-tennis table; while a more serious-minded citizen kept the hall supplied with old magazines, so enabling it to merit its title of 'Reading Room'.

Here for nearly twenty years the social life of the village was concentrated, and seldom can a village have had a livelier social life.

As focus for its activities, the Reading Room functioned as a young men's club, with a small regular subscription, sixpence a month. As such it at least provided a reasonably cosy place for the youth to foregather on winter evenings, if they were energetic enough to light the stove and the lamps. A caretaker was employed to rake out the ashes, lay the fire and fill the lamps with oil. In summer the building served as an ideal venue for cricket teas, the cricket field being just around the back. It was also patronized by the Women's Institute (started in the 1920s) and used for the village flower show and occasional events such as village teas to celebrate jubilees and coronations and for private parties and wedding receptions. The Reading Room amply fulfilled its founders' vision of an all-purpose village centre.

The bus service which now took Pitton children to grammar schools and Pitton wage-earners to jobs in Salisbury also offered a door to the world of entertainment. For the first time villagers were able to go to town on Saturday evenings to visit the Playhouse (which offered a variety programme on the lines of 'Old Time Music Hall') or the cinema. Imaginations were fired. Pitton, like many other villages, had a long history of providing its own entertainments, so why should it not emulate these new forms to which it was being introduced?

Emanuel Parsons' diaries tell of Christmas concerts at which he himself sometimes contributed solos, but these were almost exclusively at Farley. In both villages the schools were the only buildings available for secular concerts; the chapel anniversary services tended towards religious concerts. Farley too possessed, in The Wardenry, a spacious house which lent itself to parties. Here resided the vicar of Pitton and Farley, by virtue of his secondary office of warden of the endowed almshouses. In the 1920s and 1930s an old bachelor vicar, the Reverend C.M. Gay, regularly invited his parishioners, from both villages, to a much-appreciated New Year's party at The Wardenry, a function which the Pitton residents were able to attend in comfort by hiring a bus.

One of the first flowerings of the new age was the Bubbles Concert Party, founded by a group of young people to present a variety programme similar to what they had seen at the Salisbury Playhouse, had read about in the papers and had heard on the wireless. They were fortunate in having the services of an exceedingly versatile pianist and producer, Eric Bell, who worked up a lively and sophisticated entertainment not only for Pitton but for a wide circle of other villages. In those years the village was also blessed with a succession of glamorous young schoolteachers who entered enthusiastically into the world of entertainment. Predictably some of them married local lads. With all their sophistication, however, the programmes always included that traditional feature of village entertainment, the dialect comedian – here Puzzle Collins, who performed to perfection.

The change in the status of women initiated by the war was dramatic, and nowhere more so than in villages. Women who had pitched sheaves, hoed turnips, harnessed horses and generally done men's work in the fields were not inclined to return tamely to their former way of life. The emancipation thus begun was demonstrated most emphatically by women's dress.

The picture of the chapel Sunday School outing to Amesbury in 1912 or 1913 reveals the women dressed in the full ornate finery of Edwardian convention. That of an outing to the seaside fifteen years later shows the girls in short dresses above their knees, bucket hats or berets, and legs encased in the new-style silk stockings, and with shoes instead of button boots. In Victorian and Edwardian times cosmetics were frowned on, though daring lasses experimented with rose-petals for rouge and various substitutes for face powder. Now powder and lipstick were commonplace. So were perms. The profession of ladies' hairdresser did not exist, except for the gentry, at the beginning of the century, and few village women ever took scissors to their hair. Many of them took pride in being able to sit on it when they let it down at night. But now permanent waves were in high demand, and hairdressers' establishments sprang up like mushrooms to meet it.

The girls of the first decade of the century were delighted to visit a splendid little haberdashery store in Salisbury known as the Penny Bazaar – nothing more than a penny. It was later, apparently, taken over by Marks & Spencer. After the war it was joined or rivalled by Woolworth's – nothing over sixpence. No longer was there any need for the village housewives to send mysterious notes by carrier to clothiers' shops in town. A short bus journey would take them direct to the Aladdin's cave of fashionable clothes off the peg.

As for the men, casual wear gradually replaced the stiff old outfits: shirts with collars attached, often worn open-necked, blazers and sports jackets, shoes instead of solid boots, wellingtons, as already mentioned, and later those monstrous fashions – double-breasted suits and Oxford bags!

As the generation of grammar school boys and girls matured, local entertainment at the Reading Room blossomed exuberantly. From the mid-1930s to the outbreak of war the Christmas party was a notable feature of village life. Everyone was invited, and very few declined. The programme included lots of old traditional games as well as stage items and ended with community singing. Swarms of housewives spent days preparing for the feast.

PROGRAMME
of the events at

PITTON
CARNIVAL - - -

Pitton
cE.
PROGRAMME
FOR
CORONATION DAY
MAY 12TH
1937

WANT WITS' WEEKLY & PITTON SCANDALMONGER

PRICE TWOPENCE

PRICE TWOPENCE

OCTOBER 10th

WAYFARERS EN ROUTE

A party of Romanies, consisting of two bands invaded the village from the north last Sunday. As they passed along High Street and came up the hill they were watched from every window by anxious eyes. A determined assault was made on Model Farm but Mrs M. White bought them off with a pail of water.

The Gipsies pitched their camp in a strip of shingle by Webbs Corner and turned their two horses, which

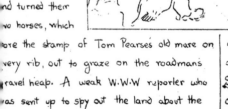

bore the stamp of Tom Pearses old mare on every rib, out to graze on the roadmans gravel heap. A weak W.W.W reporter who was sent up to spy out the land about the ninth watch (Monday morning) writes as follows —

"As for the children their name was legion. One was yelling, and three or four others were preparing to act as echoes. The men of the tribe were busy shaping the hafts of battle axes or cutting out wire-plugs or pegs, I couldn't make out which. A couple of fires were blazing and the young Ishmaels began to execute a war-dance around them. Then a woman came up and offered me a pair of bootlaces to go and hang myself with, which I did accordingly."

Later in the morning the wanderers folded up their tents like the Arabs and silently stole away.

* * * * * *

HARVEST FESTIVAL

Another batch of thankful people raised a few more songs of harvest home at St Peters' Church last Sunday and the preceeding Thursday. Rev • came down from Winterslow to preach at the week-night service, and Rev C·M· Gay officiated as usual on Sunday. The Church was decorated by willing helpers, but next year they would be well advised not to put too many apples in the windows near which the Bunkhouse Boys sit.

(Continued).

Around the same time thoughts began to turn towards acquiring a better village hall than the old Army hut, which was showing signs of wear. A fund was started, and money-raising events quickly followed. One was the village carnival, first held in 1936, when Hilda Pearce (who afterwards married the author) was elected by ballot as the first Carnival Queen.

Another, started in the previous year, was the village newspaper. Its perpetrators were a group of boys, mostly at Bishop Wordsworth School, who assembled on winter evenings in an old shepherd's hut and hence called themselves 'The Bunkhouse Boys'. Acquiring an old jelly-based duplicator, which they soon afterwards replaced by a rotary model, they set about producing a scandalsheet entitled, with typical schoolboy humour, *The Want-Wit's Weekly* or *Pitton Scandalmonger*. Although in many respects it was a typical schoolboy production, it now provides an invaluable window on the life of the times, and it is redeemed from mediocrity by the splendid little illustrations by Philip Whitlock, a talented artist who also supplied much of the text.

An event which seems to have passed without much comment at the time but which has subsequently had much to do with 'putting Pitton on the map' was the granting of a licence to sell alcoholic beverages to the off-licence run by the Eyres family. Ivyclad Farm was now the property of Percy Lampard. His application went through smoothly, and Pitton again had a pub.

Naturally the event was discussed in the Reading Room, especially as Eric Bell, who was a talented artist as well as a musician, had the commission to paint a sign for the new inn. But what should be the name? 'The Plough' seemed appropriate but rather stark and plain. The author thinks it was he who suggested 'The Silver Plough'. Or was it because Eric had a supply of silver paint? Anyway, 'The Silver Plough' it became.

Pitton was a cricketing village. Now and again it mustered a football team in winter, but from the mid-1920s onwards it had a full fixture list from May to early August inclusive. After harvest started, it was difficult to get a team together. This situation was an improvement on the state of affairs towards the end of the nineteenth century, when cricket matches could be arranged only before the beginning of haymaking or after the end of harvest. There was a tradition that a local Derby, between Pitton and the neighbouring Farley, was held in early October. Most of the matches were with neighbouring villages or Salisbury teams.

In the nineteenth century Pitton had had a Slate Club, a primitive kind of insurance society but of decidely limited scope. Records were kept on a slate, which was wiped clean once a year, when any balance left in the kitty was spent on a binge for members. The scene of this orgy, which may well have had its roots far back in the past, was the meadow known as Club Close, next to the chapel, and the occasion was always Whit Monday. When the club lapsed, the chapel took over the festival, using it for its Whitsuntide Sunday School Anniversary, when an outdoor tea, with sports, was held in Club Close.

In the gap between haymaking and harvest both church and chapel outings had to be fitted, and, from 1936 to 1939, the village Carnival.

An unchanging tradition was that of going to Salisbury Fair in October. This three-day fair, held from time out of mind, was one of the two occasions (the other being Eastertime) when almost all villagers made a special effort to go to town. The gaudy, noisy event certainly offered a complete change from routine. Prejudice against 'goin' to fair', however, existed among the more puritanical elements, though most households enjoyed nibbling the ginger-snaps, known as 'fairings', associated with the fair.

The last two months of the year were well filled with evening activities. Young people dropped in at the Reading Room most evenings, and most weeks also saw a concert, whist drive or party there.

Early November brought an important calendar event, Bonfire Night. For weeks ahead farmers brought cartloads of bushes to the brow of the hill overlooking the village, piling up a huge bonfire which was attended by most able-bodied villagers but which could, in any case, be seen by most householders from their back doors. Some families managed to acquire fireworks, but their comparative scarcity was compensated for by carbide tins, which, properly primed, produced satisfactory explosions. Juniper bushes which used to stud the hillside were gradually exterminated when the boys found that a brand from the bonfire would set them blazing fiercely.

Bonfire Night was regarded as Mischief Night, when all manner of mischief could be perpetrated with impunity. A popular sport was to collect besoms (wise housewives took their brooms indoors that night), dip them in a tar-barrel and run around brandishing them as flaming torches. Another was to push a tar-barrel to the top of the hill, set it alight and roll it down.

On one occasion, soon after the bus service had started, a gang of youths dismantled George Collins' woodpile, in the middle of the village, and built the faggots into a rampart across the road. The bus driver had to throw it down before he could pass, the next morning.

Christmas was a quiet festival – a day of relief after the long and sometimes hectic preparations. Most families enjoyed a good Christmas dinner, featuring turkey, beef, chicken or, at the least, boiled bacon from the home pig. Few if any children missed out on Christmas presents, though these were on a modest scale by modern standards. Parties were reserved for Boxing Day or the following week. The daylight hours of Boxing Day tended to be a traumatic time for the local rabbits, hares and birds, for almost every villager who possessed a gun, ferret or catapult was out after their blood.

> The busy tribes of flesh and blood,
> With all their cares and fears,
> Are carried downward by the flood,
> And lost in following years.

Many of the people encountered in 1912, at the beginning of this survey, had been swept away by the flood of time; the survivors were, by 1939, twenty-eight years older, and a new set of characters was taking over the play.

In the 1920s the era of diaries begins. In the past diaries had been kept only by the gentry and, occasionally, by their social equals. Emanuel Parsons kept a business-cum-personal diary from the 1880s to the 1920s, but he was a well-educated farmer and an estate agent as well. More representative of the village population in 1911 was old Noah White, who was barely literate. In some of his account books, from which extracts are given on pp.64-5, he set down what seemed to him some of the salient events of his lifetime. The list consists chiefly of the dates on which the springs broke in Pitton (see p.114), but a few other happenings seemed to him important.

By the late 1920s printed diaries were available for purchase and were frequently given as Christmas presents. The New Year resolution to 'keep a diary' for the coming year seldom lasted later than March, but in some instances they were kept around the year, though with extensive gaps, especially at harvest. Alice Whitlock was among the compulsive diarists, though her diaries were never more than a chronicle of events. Her son Philip tended to be more informative. However, the village diaries had few scandalous or titillating entries.

Diaries and other records, as well as living memory, have helped to make it possible to piece together the jigsaws of events between 1911 and 1939 and so to compile this narrative.

13   Words, Names and Dialect

By the 1920s and 1930s the use of the Wessex dialect was declining. Earlier generations employed it to such an extent as to be almost unintelligible to the uninitiated. In the 1920s, however, many villagers, especially the younger ones, could switch smoothly from standard English to dialect and back again to fit the company they were keeping. Dialect was used particularly on the farm, especially when talking with old farmworkers.

Two main elements were involved. The first and simplest was the use of dialect words. Although usually classified as dialect, such words have no exact counterpart in standard speech. People used them because they had nothing else to use. These are some examples:

A 'pook' is a heap of hay, twisted by a prong to make it ready for pitching onto a cart or waggon. 'To pook' is to gather up hay with a prong and twist it into a pook.

A 'knee-shy' is a baulk of timber placed across a watering-hole so that animals can drink without falling in.

The 'hames' are an essential part of a cart-horse's harness.

'Ethers' or 'edders' or 'heathers' are supple rods woven along the top of a newly laid hedge to hold the 'spleeshed' bushes in position.

'Skimmeting' or 'rough music' describes the treatment handed out by villagers to blatant adulterers, wife-beaters or other offenders against the country code.

'Raves' were the sides of a boat-waggon.

You could 'hint' a furrow, or 'split' a furrow, or plough a 'rudge' or turn a 'frommard' or a 'taillard' or do other clever things with a team of horses and a plough. If the horse 'lumpered', you shouted, 'Hi'st up there, you okkurd old sod!' or yelled, 'Way!' if it stepped over the traces.

You 'shriggled' peas or gooseberries; you were 'shrammed' by cold in winter, and the backs of your hands were 'all spreethed'. If you didn't oil your wheelbarrow, it 'scrooped'. And if all this erudition confused you, you could say that you wer 'vair duddered'.

On this level, dialect was simply the use of now obsolete or obsolescent words.

More fundamental was the use of grammar, the formation of sentences and the general manipulation of the language. One basic example is the conjugation of the verb 'to be', which in standard English is highly irregular but which in the Wessex dialect conforms precisely to the rules of the game – 'I be; thou bist; he be.' As a matter of fact, though, Wessex dialect speakers almost always used 'thee' instead of 'thou'. 'Where dost thee think thee bist gwaine?' or, to be even more accurate, 'Where dost thee think thee bist gwaine then you?' The word 'then' sometimes pronounced 'an', rounded off a sentence nicely; and 'you' was generally added when you were addressing a person directly. Dialect speakers often completed a sentence with the cryptic expression, 'sno you?' It is simply an abbreviation of the phrase, 'Dost thee know, you?'

'Do' is used as auxiliary verb far more than in standard English. 'I do cut my taties avore plantin' 'em, and then I do put em in wi' a setting-stick.' But if the man was talking about his neighbour, he would say, 'Her doth cut ees taties avore plantin', and then her doth put em in wi' a settin'-stick.' Always 'her', by the way, though goodness knows why. One old countryman told me that it was correct to use 'her' about everything except a tom-cat; that was always 'he'!

For those unfamiliar with the dialect, difficulties were increased by the use of the negative. 'I can not' and 'he can not' were commonly rendered 'I can't' and 'he can't', as in everyday English, but when addressing a person directly the old rules of grammar were strictly applied. You didn't say 'You can't'; the correct wording was 'thou canst not', with 'thee' instead if 'thou'. This was abbreviated to 'thee' cassen'. From which arose the shibboleth which dialect speakers used to test their acquaintances: 'Thee cassen see's well as thee coo'st, ca'st?' to which was often added, 'An' if thee coo'st, thee oosen!'

For any readers who cannot interpret that sentence, it reads, 'You can't see as well as you could, can you? And if you could, you wouldn't!'

In Wessex dialect an initial 'w' was often lost. You spoke of a 'ood', not a 'wood'. But it was retained for 'wheat', which was 'whate', and added gratuitously for 'oats', which were 'whuts'.

Dialect faded gradually. When half the rural populace was illiterate, it was the only speech they knew. As children they listened to what their elders said and copied them. Sometimes they got it wrong. An illiterate farmworker in the 1930s asked a farmer for some 'goosemence' seed for planting. It took the farmer some time to fathom that what he wanted was some seed potatoes of the variety 'Toogood's Tremendous'. But if people didn't pronounce their words clearly, what could he do? He couldn't check by reading.

Noah White once got a draper's assistance in Salisbury completely fogged, to the annoyance of both of them. Having failed to obtain the exact size of hat he was wishing to buy, he concluded, 'Aw well, neeshta-can, an.' Fortunately a countryman familiar with the dialect was present in the shop and was able to intervene and translate. What Noah was saying was: 'Ah well, nighest [nearest] you can, then.'

The Wessex dialect is, of course, directly derived from the old West Saxon speech. In the time of Alfred the Great and the Saxon kings who had their capital at Winchester, it was the equivalent of standard English, what is now regarded as standard English being a dialect used in the Thames Valley. When in the 1930s secondary schoolboys from the villages began to exchange visits with boys from other European countries, the visitors from Germany and the Netherlands found they could understand the local dialect better than they could standard English.

One strong factor in the survival of dialect was the Authorized Version of The Bible, with its insistence on the 'eth' ending to verbs: 'He maketh me to lie down in green pastures; he leadeth me beside the still waters.' To an illiterate countryman it seemed that that *must* be the right usage. Generations of chapel folk heard from the pulpit every Sunday local preachers using language very similar to their common speech of farmyard and field.

In a community as isolated and self-contained as Pitton in the centuries up to 1911, minutiae are magnified. For people who, as recounted in a previous chapter, seldom went farther from their native village than the nearest town, Salisbury, every detail of their home environment was important. Every tree, every bush, every plot of land, every domestic animal, was familiar to them. Even the schoolboys could unerringly find their way around the dark meadows and paddocks on moonless winter nights. They knew exactly where in the network of hedges to find the gaps – a facet of knowledge which could have proved very valuable to those of them who were later enrolled in the Home Guard, if ever Hitler's invasion had become a reality.

It did not seem unreasonable therefore for a gap in a field hedge half-way up White Way to have a name – Winser's Gap. No one could remember who Winser was, but he had evidently once lived in Pitton long enough to imprint his name on the local map. At the other end of the village the last field by Winterslow Hollow, before the old road passed into Winterslow parish, was commonly known as Genesis. In the 1920s villagers speculated idly about the derivation of the name and concluded it was a play on the fact that it was the first field in the parish, as the Book of Genesis was the first in the Bible. The discovery of an old map put an end to conjecture. 'Genesis' was simply a corruption of 'Jenningses'! – though here again no one knew who Jennings was or how long ago he lived.

White Way, White Hill, The Green and Bottom Way have obvious derivations, as have Winterslow Hollow and Farley Lane. – also, though in a slightly different category, Dirty Lane. 'Bove Hedges' has already been explained (p.000).

Cockroad, according to etymologists, was a lane where medieval villages set nets for woodcock. Woodcock are still quite numerous in woods in the neighbourhood, though the environs of Cockroad are now arable land.

Slate Way requires some explanation. The word is a contraction of 'Slay-gate Way' – the 'gate' being the entrance to the Clarenden estate. One can imagine that it commemorates a triumphant conclusion of some medieval hunt, but the reality is much more mundane. 'Slay' is a corruption of 'slae' or 'sloe', and the Slay-gate was simply the gate near which sloes were abundant. And, as a matter of fact, in the 1920s they still were.

Dunley Hill, nearby, is a definite echo from antiquity, for the etymologists derive the name from 'Dane lea' – 'Dane's meadow'. Cold Harbour, as has already been noted, should denote the presence of a ruined Roman villa, where a traveller could find cold lodgings, but no such villa site has ever been found, though an explanation

has been suggested (see p.100). Nemett's Lane is highly
suggestive. Incidentally, the name 'Abbot's Close' noted
in previous chapters should, according to some old-time
villagers, be 'Nobbus's Close'. The adding to or omission
from place-names of an 'n' is a common feature of Saxon
etymology, so it is difficult to say which version is correct.
Around the beginning of the century an iron turnstile
known as the Whorley-Gog marked the junction of
Abbot's Close and the Street, but it has long since been
demolished.

In the modern village the housing estates of Beeches'
Close and Elm Close have recently invented names, but
David's Garden is a name from the past, so distant that the
identity of David has been forgotten. The use of 'the
Street' for the main throughfare and of 'Townsend' for the
termination of the village are both evidences of
considerable antiquity.

Some names derived from former owners of land
endured for a time and then faded away. It is recorded
that James Webb, who lived at Webb's Farm in the middle
of the eighteenth century, farmed a considerable acreage
of fields scattered about the parish. Of those to which his
name was attached, Webb's Down, describing the fields in
the eastern part of the parish, towards Hound Wood,
which were once downland, is still remembered. Webb's
Bottom, referring to a shallow valley at the top end of
Parsonage Farm, is, however, a name no longer used.

Whether a place-name survives for centuries or is soon
forgotten seems to be entirely fortuitous. A medieval
document catalogues the boundaries of Clarendon Forest
in the year 1300. On the eastern side of the estate,
adjoining Pitton, the names are as follows: Holeway,
Muleford, Pynkelway, Wyldeneditch, Schireveswood,
Rutheresheved, Stolkewey, Slaygate of Putton, Rodesle,
Langhimeswey, Odesle, Howe, Stoneysgore.

Of them, Mulford is the village or suburb of Milford.
Wyldeneditch is the deer-leap, still traceable, along the
edge of the present forested area of the Clarendon estate;
Schireves Wood, though no longer a wood, is attached to a
field near White Way – it was once Sherriff's Wood;

Slaygate of Putton has already been described (p.82); Howe is a field by Cockroad, at a point where the Pitton, Farley and Clarendon lands meet. And all the intervening landmarks have been forgotten. It seems a pity that such an attractive name as Pynkelewey should have vanished!

Imagine a stranger arriving in Pitton in the second half of the nineteenth century and asking for Mr Whitlock.

'Which Mr Whitlock? There are nineteen of them – more, if you count the unmarried chaps.'

'Well, Mr George Whitlock.'

Then he would discover, as family genealogists have discovered, to their utter confusion, that there were two Mr George Whitlocks, of about the same age, each married to a wife named Elizabeth and producing their families more or less simultaneously!

The villagers solved the problem to their satisfaction by awarding nicknames. 'Billy Lazarus' is one already mentioned. Often people were known by their maternal surnames. Three full brothers were respectively known as Joe Pearce, Jess Head and Arth Whitlock. Whitlock was their real surname, Pearce was their mother's maiden name, and Head was their paternal grandmother's maiden name.

By the 1920s new elements were creeping in, though nicknames were as popular as ever. The cinema was making its first impact. Parents had not yet got around to naming their offspring after film stars, but boys were quick to pick out appropriate nicknames for their schoolmates. An early film star was 'Fatty' Arbuckle, so that seemed a natural nickname for a boy a little on the plump side. It soon became shortened to 'Buckie' and the derivation was forgotten. The author's nickname used even by his mother, was 'Coguey', arrived at by the following circumlocutory chain of thought: a simple corruption of 'Ralph' was 'Japhet', which by usage became 'Jackie', and Jackie Coogan was a popular film star. An unlikely sequence, but true.

Other nicknames of the 1920s were 'Steppy', 'Mousey', 'Pip', 'Puzzle', 'Little-un', 'Barmy', 'Clinger' and 'Kelly'.

But by the 1930s the cult of nicknames seemed to have largely died out.

In the 1910s and 1920s, as the exploits of those popular Victorian heroes penetrated even to this remote village, Stanley and Gordon began to be used as Christian names, and until then David (from David Livingstone) was hardly known, which lends support to the idea that the place-name 'David's Garden' was originally 'Davy's Garden', Davy being a surname.

14 *Birds, Beasts and Flowers*

After the Sale the situation regarding game (see pp.25, 62) altered. The new tenants of the County Council Smallholdings Committee formed a kind of syndicate to rent the shooting rights and re-let them to the Clarendon estate. The difference between the rent they paid and the rent they received provided a small but welcome addition to their income. The incentive to poach on most of the Pitton farms was thus removed, and in general the tenants played fair. Hares, however, were excluded from the agreement, and hares were much more numerous than they are today.

The countryside swarmed with rabbits. They were

everywhere. On the downs to the north of the village they could be seen scampering about or sunning themselves in their hundreds in broad daylight, and it is an axiom that for every rabbit visible there are at least ten underground or in the bushes. The annual holocaust of rabbits at harvest-time was one of the features of farm life. The mode of procedure at harvest was for the binder to cut the standing corn by travelling in ever-decreasing circles until only a narrow strip was left in the middle of the field. This strip would be alive with rabbits, which now dashed out in all directions. The farmer stood in a strategic position with his double-barrelled 12-bore gun but was frustrated in his attempts to use it by the presence of dozens of excited men, boys and dogs chasing dodging rabbits, which probably had a 50:50 chance of escaping. When the massacre was over, the rabbits, and an occasional hare, were laid out on the stubbles and allocated by the farmers to every participant. The unwritten law was that everyone who joined in the mêlée should have a share, the farmer taking the remainder. Even so, there were usually so many that it was said that in a poor crop the rabbits yielded more than the corn.

Incessant war was waged against the rabbit population, with little effect on their numbers. The losses incurred in arable crops by rabbits nibbling away acres of grain around the headlands were proportionately enormous. In their warfare the villagers, even the most pious, were curiously insensitive about cruelty. They used the barbarous gin-traps freely, and every boy learnt at an early age how and where to set wire snares. Ferreting was also a popular recreation on Saturday afternoons.

In the first years after taking the tenancy of the down farm (230 acres) in 1934, Ted Whitlock paid the rent in rabbits, killing about 2,000 a year and still making little apparent impact on their numbers. His favourite method of dealing with them was by Saturday afternoon shoots, the rabbits being so numerous that they tended to lie up in bushes rather than occupy the overcrowded burrows. The dogs had a wonderful time.

Deer were also fairly plentiful in the woodlands, though

not nearly as numerous as rabbits. All were fallow deer, the now common roe deer being hardly known. In winter they raided farmsteads, pulling hay from hayricks and digging mangolds from root-clamps. Farmers and poachers sometimes set wires for them – wire clothes lines, in fact – but very seldom caught one. The fallow deer population flourished until war-time, when they were rounded up and their carcases sold in Salisbury market.

Foxes were in an enigmatic situation. The farmers regarded them as mortal enemies, and their nuisance value was indeed very considerable, as shutting up fowl-houses each night and opening them each morning when the hens were on free range occupied an hour or two every day. Every farmer was prepared to shoot a fox if he could do it surreptitiously. On the other hand, it was policy to keep on good terms with the local hunt, to whom claims for compensation could be addressed in the event of a poultry massacre.

Pitton had at least one badger sett. Of lesser mammals, rats and mice were abundant, even the attractive little golden-brown harvest mouse being not uncommon. The red squirrel had not yet been replaced in the woods by grey squirrels, and they were plentiful enough to have a popular name – 'scuggies'.

Moles were known as 'wants', and shrews as 'over-runners', from their alleged mischief in causing a cow's milk to dry by running over her udders when she was lying down. Hedgehogs were likewise unpopular, for the reason that they were said to suck milk from sleeping cows. They anyway fell frequent victims to traps set in hedges. Bats were 'flittermice'.

Birds had a hard time trying to survive in the old-time village. For the past century or two the pheasant had reigned supreme, and any creature capable or thought to be capable of preying on it (except foxes) was ruthlessly eliminated by zealous gamekeepers. Birds with hooked beaks and talons, notably hawks and owls, were regarded as arch-enemies. Every keeper had a gibbet where their dying carcases were displayed, for his employers to see and pay tribute to his efficiency.

A similar interdict lay on all members of the crow family, especially jays and magpies. Many keepers operated the detestable pole-traps, baited with eggs, for jays. Some old-timers remember walking in the woods after Sunday School on Sunday afternoons and being distressed by the screams of a jay dangling by the leg from a gin-trap on a pole. They wanted to go and release it but were deterred by the likelihood of getting into trouble with the keeper, who held the theory that the bird's tortured cries would scare away other jays – a fallacy: they were more likely to attract them.

Rooks were held to be the farmers' enemies, on the grounds that they feasted on newly sown grain. Their usefulness in feeding on leatherjackets, wireworms and other insect pests was not appreciated. Wood pigeons, of course, were much more destructive and were shot whenever possible but have always been well able to take care of themselves.

Lapwings, or peewits as they known locally, were more plentiful than at present, there being several pairs wheeling and screaming on every farm at nesting time. Their eggs were regularly collected in March and were much appreciated for breakfast, though some were sold in Salisbury. The subsequent decline of the peewit is sometimes attributed to the cessation of this practice. The early eggs, so the argument goes, were nearly all chilled through the mother bird being absent too long when disturbed by farm workers ploughing, harrowing, sowing or rolling the fields. When the eggs were collected, the birds set about laying another clutch which, cultivations being by then over (no sowing of fertilizer or spraying!), they were able to incubate and hatch without interruption. When the early eggs were *not* collected, the parent bird would return to sit on them, not realizing that they had become chilled, and by the time she had discovered there were going to be no chicks it was too late to start again.

A bird whose decline has been more dramatic and complete than that of the peewit is the stone curlew. A smaller relation of the great bustard, which itself was once a denizen of Salisbury Plain, the stone curlews were early migrants, arriving in March and starting nesting straight away. Birds of the lonely downs and bare waste places, the derelict fields of 1910-40 suited them well, though they seem also to have favoured turnip fields.

Villagers with recollections of that period remember the stone-curlew with affection. For them it was the authentic voice of the downs. On late summer and early autumn evenings, parties of stone curlew, assembling for migration, carolled across the valley at twilight. First a choir in the fields near Piccadilly Clump would begin the evening chorus, one bird alone starting the performance and dozens then quickly joining in. When they paused, another company on the opposite hill would start up, and finally the hill group would sweep across the valley to meet the Piccadilly birds, the whole choir going at full volume. As many as seventy birds were sometimes recorded in those autumn flocks, and their crepuscular repertoire made an unforgettable experience. Stone curlew still nest in small numbers on Salisbury Plain, but none in the neighbourhood of Pitton, and it is doubtful whether they will ever again be seen or heard in such numbers.

Another bird which has vanished from the village fields, in this instance irrevocably, is the corncrake. Few villagers now living can remember hearing them, but Ted Whitlock testified to the fact that in the 1880s and 1890s they were abundant. Their raucous calls were as familiar as the notes of the cuckoo, and they teemed in every hayfield. Their disappearance is often blamed on the introduction of the mechanical grasscutter in lieu of the scythe but, though this may well have been a contributory factor, it does not seem entirely satisfactory.

In the 1930s a pair of quails used to nest regularly in a field just over the parish boundary, in what is now Firsdown. A bungalow now stands on the nesting site. Sometimes, too, a pair nested by the Drove, but these birds have not been recorded for many years.

Wheatears, which arrived in March like the stone curlews, were abundant on the downs, nesting in disused rabbit burrows. Their catastrophic and dramatic decrease has had its counterpart elsewhere. On the Sussex downs shepherds used to make a useful addition to their income by catching wheatears by the hundred on the autumn migration, while it is recorded that on the Isle of Portland, Dorset boys used to catch as many as 400 a day during harvest. They caught them chiefly in horsehair nooses in stone traps or at the entrance to rabbit burrows and sold them to visitors at threepence a dozen. Although no such trade existed at Pitton, the birds were certainly plentiful on the downs. Now years pass without any being seen.

Nearly related to the wheatear, the stonechat was a familiar companion to shepherds around the sheepfolds in autumn and winter, though now seldom seen. Red-backed shrikes were common enough to be given a local name, 'high mountain sparrows'. Their decline seems to have been nationwide, for at the same period W.H. Hudson reported them quite common around London. None has been recorded in or near Pitton for many years.

No birds had an easy life in the village of the period under review. Even the smallest ones were subject to the predatory activities of small boys, unchecked by their elders. Some 'sports' were traditional. On winter evenings gangs of boys roamed farmyards, extracting sparrows and tits from their roosting holes in thatched eaves. In this activity they were encouraged or at least tolerated by the farmers, who regarded sparrows in particular as pests.

Less favoured by the farmers and indulged in only surreptitiously by the boys was to set a lantern in the middle of a barn, open the barn doors and beat the thatch of the adjacent buildings. The birds naturally flew towards the light where they were set upon by whooping, boisterous boys with clubs, who were as likely to hit each other or the lantern as the birds.

A similar method was to set a boy walking with a lantern behind a tall net carried by two other boys alongside a tall hedge where finches and buntings were known to roost. More boys on the other side of the hedge beat the bushes and made ample commotion, which sent the disturbed birds flying straight into the net.

Yet another similar strategy was the daytime operation known as 'squolling'. A gang of boys walked on either side of a dense hedge, looking for birds in it. When they found one, usually a skulking blackbird, they surrounded it and started to pelt it with stones and sticks or to use their catapults. Thrushes would rise to the tops of the bushes and fly away, but blackbirds invariably stayed in the bottom of the hedge, trying to escape by moving from bush to bush – often fatal tactics.

These were mostly gang operations, but in addition most boys practised solitary methods of catching birds, such as by horsehair nooses (often laid in threshing rubbish where many birds fed) and brick-traps.

Their activities were made more lethal by the introduction of airguns, which seem to have been acquired by most village boys in the 1920s, doubtless as Christmas or birthday presents from parents who ought to have known better. 'Squolling' now became nearly as hazardous for the boys as for the birds, and almost anything served for target practice.

An early attempt at diary-keeping by a fourteen-year-old lad in 1929 develops into little more than a record of game bag, the game being small birds. Sample: '*January 9th* Today I shot 8 blackbirds, 2 thrushes, 2 starlings, 1 lark and 1 bullfinch.' To this was added a minor redeeming feature: 'I caught a robin in a brick-trap and let it go.' Robins and swallows were immune from the general massacre. If you killed one of these birds or took their eggs, your little finger grew crooked.

On reflection, though, the boys were only emulating their elders. On 9 January the fourteen-year-old noted that his father shot two pigeons. And only a couple of decades earlier Lord Ilchester travelled up from Dorset for a day's sport measured by the items in the game bags: '24 pheasants, 8 brace partridges, 29 rabbits, 4 hares, 1 woodcock.'

Vivid memories of the hungry years of the nineteenth century were still retained. For countrymen then, blackbirds were ingredients for pies (*vide*, the nursery rhyme), as were sparrows, larks, wheatears and any other small birds. Meat in general was so scarce that the small morsels of breast meat on these feathered miniscules were worth the trouble of killing, plucking and dressing them. People still living have eaten blackbird pie or toasted larks spitted on a skewer. A book entitled *The Wild Foods of Great Britain*, first published in 1917, recommends recipes for cooking all the small birds mentioned, as well as moorhens, peewits, wheatears and gulls. Starlings need to have their heads cut off immediately they are killed, says the author, and this was a precaution well known in Pitton. Only *young* rooks, just fledged, were fit to eat.

Several cottagers kept song-birds, such as goldfinches, bullfinches and linnets, in small cages, and old Noah Whitlock is remembered as using bird-lime and taking young goldfinches from nests, presumably for sale as cage-birds.

It is providential that the lovely little collared doves, now such a familiar feature of English villages, didn't try to make their spectacular irruption from south-eastern Europe sixty years earlier. Arriving in England in the 1920s, they wouldn't have stood a chance.

Rabbits were not the only creatures to infest in their scores and even hundreds the last strip of standing corn at harvest-time. Fields on the edge of the chalk downs were often alive with butterflies, especially blue ones. Chalk-hill blues and Adonis blues, as well as the common and small blues, were abundant. These marginal barleyfields were an entomologist's paradise, as were also the floors of the harvest waggons immediately after a load of sheaves had been removed. They provided a cross-section of every species of caterpillar, beetle and other insect living among the cornstalks.

Certain wild flowers now rare flourished in the neglected countryside of the 1920s and 1930s. In the woods the system of coppicing every seven or eight years, with the associated clearance of weeds and brambles, left a clean woodland floor on which primroses, anemones, woodruff, orchids and bluebells could thrive with little competition. On the impoverished downs nutrients were so scarce that coarse grasses and other vegetation had no chance of smothering the lowly but exquisite little downland flowers such as milkwort, fairy flax, wild thyme, squinancy-wort, rock-rose, bird's foot trefoil, eyebright and harebell, as well as bee orchids, fragrant orchids, pyramid orchids, green man orchids and burnt orchids. Cowslips were so abundant in the meadows that schoolchildren were encouraged to gather them in quantities for making 'cowslip balls', by snipping off their heads and tying them into a ball with wool.

When hoeing was the only method of controlling weeds, many now rare flowers of cultivated land were plentiful. Cornfields were as red with poppies as paintings by romantic artists depict them, and the now rare magenta-coloured corncockle grew along the field edges. Brilliant patches of mustard yellow on the farm landscape would indicate fields infested with charlock, not a good crop of oilseed rape. A parasite which has now almost completely disappeared was dodder, which in times past had been a major problem on clover.

This chapter would be hardly complete without mention of the welfare of domestic animals. As with humans in medieval centuries and earlier, their first illness was generally their last one. The alternative title of 'horse doctors' for veterinary surgeons suggests correctly that their services were confined more or less to horses, and valuable horses at that. When to call a doctor to an urgent case of human illness involved a cycle ride over six hilly miles and a corresponding journey for the doctor by carriage and trap, the likelihood of a peasant farmer calling in a vet to treat a sick animal was remote.

When horses and cows were worn out, they walked to the knacker's yard at Winterbourne. Ailing pigs and sheep were quickly despatched and eaten. Most villagers, though not all, drew the line at eating animals that had died through illness, but a sick animal killed was regarded as edible. Under the old dispensation farmers insisted that all dead or dying sheep be reported to them by the shepherd, for the reason that shepherds were often under suspicion of killing a sheep for their own use from time to time. One of the purposes for which dead sheep were in demand was the extraction of tallow for making candles. Old people alive in the 1920s could remember nocturnal expeditions to the River Avon at Alderbury where grew the giant hemlock dropwort, the hollow dead stems of which made excellent moulds for tallow candles.

Poultry (except geese) and rabbits were killed by the simple process of wringing their necks, a quick and probably painless death. Geese had to be stunned by a blow and then have their jugular vein cut. Dogs and cats, when their lives were obviously drawing to a close, were shot. The author has seen his father, tears trickling down his cheeks, take a much-loved old dog, suffering from cancer, out to the dung-heap in the yard and shoot it. It was one of the recognized duties of the head of a family.

Epilogue

Pitton is still on the map. It still occupies its ancient site in the valley that marks the boundary between woodland and what was once downland. Its thriving population is probably more numerous (around 500) than at any time in its long history. What has vanished, as effectively as a dispersing morning mist in summer, is the way of life of which it was once the scene.

Two fundamental social changes are responsible for what happened. Throughout its history until very recently Pitton was a village of peasant farmers. Agriculture has always been a labour-intensive industry. Working on a farm has always meant manual work. Traditionally, a little farm of less than 100 acres provided a livelihood for four or five families. In Pitton at the end of the nineteenth century a farm of 190 acres employed ten men, besides the farmer. Even a farm of 35 acres provided work for three labourers. In a census of those times, out of 157 employed or self-employed persons no fewer than 103 are classified as agricultural labourers.

Mechanization and specialization have completely changed the pattern. There are now eight farmers, not one of whom employs regular workers. The small amount of work the farmer himself cannot cope with he lets out to contractors. Of the other workers and craftsmen who just before the beginning of this chronicle earned their livelihood within the limits of the village and its fields, nearly all belonged to categories no longer represented. The bricklayers, carpenters, sawyers, woodmen, shoe-makers, blacksmiths, turners, hurdle-makers and brushmakers have all disappeared. Only the innkeeper and the shopkeeper remain.

So if Pitton were now relying on its home fields and its resident industries to provide a living for its inhabitants, it would be a ghost village. It would be gradually fading from the map, like the lost villages of the past.

But another mighty social change has supplied more than ample compensation. The increased mobility for which the motor car is largely responsible has made the village a highly desirable residential location. The population has been vastly augmented by newcomers who cheerfully commute thirty or forty miles daily or even to London to work. The provision of electricity, telephone and piped water, all of which the village acquired in one year (1938), has made it a cosy little nest for retired couples. And new generations of the old village families have found no reason to move out because the farms no longer provide work for them, for they too can commute by car to jobs in Salisbury or further afield. So Pitton flourishes and is more populous than ever before.

But perhaps 'village' no longer aptly describes it. 'Suburbage' maybe?

Life continued in Pitton during the Second World War much as in earlier decades. Petrol rationing and other wartime restrictions threw the village back on its own resources in a way with which the older inhabitants were entirely familiar. The ploughing-up campaign required the farmers to plough most of their worn-out meadows and to reclaim all available derelict land, a requirement which bore particularly heavily on Ted Whitlock, with his recently acquired 230 acres of downland. Harvest camps for volunteer helpers were organized, and the end of harvest saw revivals of the old-type Harvest Homes.

It took a few years after the war for the realization to circulate that Pitton was now, with all its recently acquired amenities, a decidedly attractive place to live in. Planning regulations came into force, and very many attractive old cottages, mostly thatched, were condemned and demolished because they did not conform to the official standards, such as indoor toilets and bathrooms and a proper ratio of window space to room dimensions. Said

Ted Whitlock, 'You see the suburban house our Planning Officer lives in? That's what Pitton will be like in twenty years' time.' And to a large extent he was right, though a sufficient number of the newcomers recognized the possibilities of the old cottages and, by imaginative conversion, saved some of them for posterity. Obedient, too, to the policy of in-filling, many of the new houses have been crammed into restricted spaces, thus defeating the concept of spacious living which presumably people look for when seeking a village home. Property values have of course been multiplied from twenty to a hundredfold; no real comparison can be valid because of the change in the value of money.

The only village houses or cottages available to rent now are council houses, and even they are becoming scarcer as the Government's policy of selling them to tenants bites. Some farms, though not in Pitton, have tied cottages for their workers, and a serious problem arises when a farm worker retires and his cottage is needed for his successor.

Young people thinking of getting married face a daunting prospect. A couple I was recently talking with have a joint income of rather less than £250 a week and savings of less than £1000. A village cottage is out of the question for them, and the cheapest property they could find in the back streets of Salisbury would cost around £50,000. The mortgage they would have to saddle themselves with is frightening. More than half their income just to pay the interest.

Is the village better or worse than it used to be? Not an easy question, but I would say, from the point of view of standard of life, immeasurably better. Those who yearn for the 'good old days' tend to be fantasizing. It has been said, with some justification, that life in the countryside back in Victorian and earlier times was ghastly. Well, perhaps not entirely so. We would probably think so if we were suddenly transported back there, but it must be remembered that the villagers of those times did not have our own age as a yardstick. They lived their lives in the manner to which they were born and bred, and found them tolerable.

With so few distractions, such as radio, television, videos and a raucous Press, the more intelligent villagers had more time to think. Fed largely on the Bible and its exposition heard every Sunday from the pulpit, they had perhaps a deeper spiritual awareness than most of their successors. But their religion did not often teach them to be more humane in their dealings with other life, wild and domestic, with which they shared their lovely countryside.

On the whole, human nature is much the same as it has always been. Each generation adapts to its environment and social atmosphere and develops its character accordingly. What can be said is that the village of 1910-39, as described in this book, has been irretrievably lost in the mists creeping up from the horizon.

Index